Harold 'Doc' Keen
and the
Bletchley Park BOMBE

GW00579185

Harold 'Doc' Keen

— and the —

Bletchley Park BOMBE

by

John Keen

B

M & M Baldwin
Cleobury Mortimer, Shropshire
2003

First published by M & M Baldwin in April 2003.

ISBN 0 947712 42 9

Published by
— M & M BALDWIN —
24 High St, Cleobury Mortimer,
Kidderminster DY14 8BY
email: enigma@mbaldwin.free-online.co.uk

Printed by
— FRANKLYN PUBLICITY LTD —
Park House, Hurdsfield Road, Macclesfield SK10 1LL

— Contents —

— Illustrations —

— Preface —

When World War II began, British Intelligence was unable to break into the high-security radio communciation system used throughout Germany's armed forces and which utilised the highly developed Enigma cipher machine.

But, by early September 1939, the GC&CS team at Bletchley Park had already been considerably enlarged, and included mathematicians Alan Turing and Gordon Welchman who had joined John Jeffreys, Peter Twinn and others. Within three months, Alan Turing and Gordon Welchman had evolved their own complex Enigma code-breaking method. But its usefulness depended upon the rapidity of application to each intercepted Enigma message; this demanded a largely automated and high-speed technical process.

The design and development of a suitable machine was undertaken by Harold Keen of the British Tabulating Machine Company. During the late 1930s electronic computers were unknown, and a solution required innovation and the use of existing technology in a manner not seen before.

This account traces Harold Keen's background and looks at the design approach in the creation of his machine. It records, also, the close association of the company with Bletchley Park in providing the crypyto-logists with many copies of this machine and its variants throughout the war.

Harold ('Doc') Keen's machine, code-named CANTAB, was Bletchley Park's Bombe. By the end of the war, well over 200 had been built and used by the codebreakers in their widespread breaking of the Enigma which, it is claimed, effectively shortened the duration of the war.

— Acknowledgements —

John Harper gave many corrective and additional details of the 3-rotor Bombe, and some design knowledge of the 4-rotor Bombe, as did Norman Hedges. I thank John Gallehawk for his help, and his guidance on sourcing photographs. Mrs Hilda Keen kindly made available Frank Keen's 1945 notebook. I thank Peter Howkins for his Stanmore input, and David Whitehead for his detail of the Cobra project at Eastcote.

Photos of the 3-rotor Enigma were provided by Dr Mark Baldwin, and those of the 3-rotor Bombe 'ATLANTA' by the American National Archives & Records Administration. The photo of the Bombe 'MONS' is reproduced with the permission of the Controller of HMSO.

Acknowledgements are due to John Harper and Jim Walden for providing the drawings used in Figures 5 & 6.

— Author's Note —

The development of 3-rotor Bombe covered some three years following early exploratory tests and the prototypes of 1940.

The Bombe details given in this book are generally of a later, 1942-3, version and concern the machine functions necessary to perform essential steps in the 'probable word' method of deciphering Enigma messages, outlined in Appendix 1.

Lacking are details relating to the Keen version of the 4-rotor Bombe, and to a lesser extent the Cobra version, and concern design changes to minimise the time involved with the greatly extended test routine. Available evidence might support those indicated.

— Chapter 1 —

Formative Years, 1894 – 1939

Harold Hall Keen was born into a family which had its origins in the Amersham area of Buckinghamshire, certainly his father and his mother were both from that part.

However, during the nineteenth century there had been considerable movement of individuals and families, particularly away from the country life of provincial areas to towns and cities. The Keen family had followed this general trend and, by the year 1893 at least, was living in the north London borough of Shoreditch. Here Harold was born in 1894 as the third child of the family, there already being an older brother and sister; he was to be joined, in due course, by two younger brothers.

By 1894 the nineteenth century was drawing to a close, and the stability of the Victorian era was soon to be threatened by political and social changes. In terms of technology, although innovation had steadily progressed through the century, it now began to flourish in many directions which were directly affecting everyday life. The use of electric power was soon to spread, petrol-engined automobiles were already appearing, and mechanical innovations in household appliances of all descriptions were becoming available.

Nevertheless, several advances of universal significance were yet to be realised; successful powered flight had yet to appear, and although Marconi had started experiments with radio signal transmissions, trans-Atlantic communication by radio would have to wait until after the turn of the century, and the benefits of public radio broadcasting and receiving were not to be generally available for another generation. However, the American, Samuel Morse, had already established his code for communication via overland telegraphy, and this would eventually become the universal medium to be used in wireless technology throughout the next century.

Early in the new century Harold Keen was in his teens and living in London where, undoubtedly, he was becoming aware of the changes that were taking place and which would ultimately affect his choice of career.

By his eighteenth year Harold Keen had moved into lodgings in Kentish Town, in the borough of St Pancras, probably motivated by a desire to develop his own future independently of the family. While there, he had already commenced his training in Electrical Engineering, intending to join a suitable company involved with one of the new technologies.

He had also previously developed a considerable interest in music and had decided to become a competent pianist. Having a natural talent, he was in the process of achieving this goal and, even while doing so, wished also to further apply his abilities to master the organ and its music. With this in mind, and while still in his late teens, he applied for, and was accepted in, the position of organist at St John's Church in Hoxton, Shoreditch. This appointment required him to be conveniently near at hand, which might have been an additional reason for his having taken lodgings where he had.

It is possible that he might have even considered a full-time career in music at this time, despite its inherent vagaries. However, he decided against this step, and instead sought an engineering job, though remaining determined to pursue music for the enjoyment it provided.

He was attracted to a young engineering company that had been formed in 1902 to build the mechanised accounting machines developed and patented by an American, Herman Hollerith.[1*] It was clearly a company involved with a new technology and in 1912 he joined the company as a young engineer.

From that time onward engineering and music were to become two prime motivations in his life, both during his bachelor years and after marriage.

---

* See pages 85-89 for notes.

The company that he joined, 'The Tabulator Limited', was established in London with offices in Norfolk Street, off the Strand, and had engineering workshops in Watford and Great Saffron Hill, London. The company had been formed to import and assemble equipment manufactured by The Tabulating Machine Company (TMC) in the United States and which incorporated the 'punched card' accounting methods patented in the 1880s by Herman Hollerith. With his original company, 'The Hollerith Electric Tabulating Company', Hollerith was awarded the contract to mechanise the American census of 1890 with his punched card system. Processing and publishing the results of the American census of 1880 had taken seven years. By 1890 the population had doubled, essentially a result of heavy immigration, and a mechanical form of handling the census information became necessary.[2]

The Ex-Director of Census, Robert Porter, subsequently moved to England to set up an English company and obtain the rights to the TMC patents and to import their machines under licence. This he succeeded in doing in 1902 and formed 'The Tabulator Ltd', with himself as chairman. Ralegh Phillpotts was appointed as part-time joint general manager with Everard Green who was a trained engineer. One of several financial backers was Sir Gerald Chadwick Healey. The company's registered office was at 2 Norfolk Street.[3]

Hollerith's punched card system was one of three inventions, the others being typewriters and calculators, that had changed the American office environment from 1890 onwards.[4] However, it took some ten years for these innovations to cross the Atlantic, and by the far-sightedness of its founder members, The Tabulator Ltd was to participate directly in the future mechanisation of business in England.

The company's first trial machine installation was at the Woolwich Arsenal; this ended in complete failure when the machines were repeatedly sabotaged and eventually forced out by a reactionary office staff who felt threatened by the coming of mechanisation. But success followed and by 1907 the company was renamed The British Tabulating Machine Company Limited (BTM) and, in 1910, was awarded the contract to mechanise the 1911 British census under the control of a consultant engineer, G H Ballie.[5] To meet this commitment, extra staff were appointed including Harry Waters as works manager. By 1912 Harold Keen had also joined the company.

During 1911 the American TMC merged with other office product companies in the USA to form 'The Computing, Tabulating and Recording Company', (CTR). In 1914 Thomas J Watson became President of CTR whose name was changed to 'International Business Machines', (IBM), and which, during the 1920s and 1930s, was to become outstandingly successful in the realm of business machinery.[6]

Following the outbreak of the First World War in 1914 a number of staff joined the services, including Ralegh Phillpotts. For the next year Harold Keen remained with the company, but in 1916 he joined the Royal Flying Corps and was posted to the ground staff of a bomber squadron in northern France. The time he spent in maintaining the early aircraft and equipment in harsh conditions probably gave him an increased knowledge of engine ignition systems, electric generators, and the like, and an awareness at first hand of the strengths and weaknesses that can occur in practical engineering. When his service in the RFC ended in 1919 he returned to civilian life and rejoined BTM. In the same year, aged twenty-six, he married Eva Burningham whom he had known for some years. They were married in the church of St John, Hoxton, where he had previously been organist.

BTM had had a successful and expanding business during the war with orders from government munitions and aeroplane factories, and the armed forces. This success continued after 1919 during the economic boom of 1919-1920 and the mechanised office was becoming the norm in commercial businesses. BTM decided to set up its own manufacturing operation. This required more staff, office accommodation and workshop space. Suitable premises were not available in London and so in 1920 the company moved out of London to a new site in the small town of Letchworth in north Hertfordshire and there built a new factory.[7]

Letchworth, the first 'Garden City', was based upon the ideas of Ebenezer Howard, and was founded in 1903. By 1920 the town was attracting manufacturing companies to settle there with the prospect of modern conditions and a local workforce. In 1921 the company's new factory was opened and the majority of the London staff moved to Letchworth, including Harold Keen and his family.

Being a young company, BTM had avoided the restrictive industrial attitudes that existed in some well-established companies. In a more open business and engineering environment that followed there developed a harmonious relationship amongst the company staff which continued throughout the period of the original founders. In addition, many companies at this time were in a period of innovative mentality, including both BTM and IBM. Harold Keen was, by nature, well suited to this environment. During his early years in the company he was already applying himself with enthusiasm. As a young engineer he was spending much of his time travelling between home, the engineering works and customer installations and carrying paper-work, tools and minor technical items. To carry these he used a small case similar to, or possibly an actual, doctor's bag, then in common use. Because of this habit his fellow engineers came to refer to him as 'Doctor Keen'. This, reduced to 'Doc Keen', became the name he was known by during his time with BTM, generally throughout the company, and elsewhere.

Very soon after the company moved to Letchworth he joined a small team to visit the company's offices and customer installations in India as part of a periodic assessment of BTM's overseas business, including several of the more commercially developed parts of the Empire. This visit took some ten months to complete and took him to various company offices and installations in India's major cities. From that time on, he also became the company representative at Engineering Association meetings and European conferences, mostly held during that time in Paris and Geneva.

He was appointed head of an Experimental Department when it was founded in 1923 and during the years that followed he was eventually to became regarded as the most successful innovator of British punched card machinery.

By 1930, with a staff numbering 350, BTM was preparing to undertake its own serious design work.[8] Harold Keen had already become responsible for the development of new designs, and during the ensuing years he was granted over sixty technical patents. He eventually became Chief Engineer in the 1930s and started the design of new advanced machines which became standard products until the late 1950s.

As his life progressed Keen continued to indulge his musical interests and expand his activities. During the 1920s and early 1930s he had created and conducted the 'Tab Choir', within the company, for both male and female members of the staff; later on he would also provide pleasure to himself and to others with his Sunday afternoon organ recitals, sponsored by a Miss Lawrence who was at that time one of the remaining 'first' Letchworthians.

He continued his organ music in churches of various denominations as opportunities arose, and extended this activity by becoming a choirmaster, perhaps encouraged by his earlier experience with the Tab Choir.

By the late 1930s the Company was conducting business in all major Commonwealth countries with the exception of Canada; at home most government Ministries and the armed services, as well as the majority of the larger commercial companies, and many smaller, had mechanised their accountancy with BTM equipment. By now BTM's staff had reached a total of over 1000; of the original nucleus of its staff, Ralegh Phillpotts had become Chairman of the company, G H Ballie was Managing Director, and Everard Green a member of the Board. Harry Waters was manager of the Manufacturing Works and Harold Keen had already become Chief Engineer and Head of Design & Development.

By 1939 Europe was in a state of disruption and facing the likelihood of war. Following its occupation of Austria in 1938 and, later, Czechoslovakia, Germany was threatening Poland. Letchworth, like many other towns and cities had, since 1938, become a haven for refugees from the affected areas of Europe and their numbers were increasing. As the year 1939 progressed, daily BBC news bulletins started to include call-up notices for reservists of the armed forces as the country prepared for an uncertain future.

The declaration of war on September 3 was to have a considerable impact on Doc Keen's future. By the following November he and BTM were to become closely involved with resolving the problem presented to British Intelligence by the Enigma machine used by the Germans for encrypting the majority of their radio-transmitted communications throughout their armed forces. This became his predominant wartime activity and the company's increasing involvement eventually commanded nearly a third of its resources.

— Chapter 2 —

Enigma

Germany started the war with its armed forces equipped with an efficient and highly organised radio communication system using Morse-coded message transmissions. To provide high security for these transmissions they had adopted during the 1920s a mechanised encryption system based on the Enigma machine which they had developed from its original commercial design.

Before Hitler came to power in 1932, the size of the professional army was already being increased. The highly mechanised army and the airforce, intended to be the spearhead in later wars, were to have sophisticated radio communication systems. These would need security ciphers for protection. By 1933 Enigma had been adopted as the cipher system for the armed forces, military intelligence, SS, the Nazi Party security and political intelligence service. The discovery that Germany had adopted an apparently unbreakable machine cipher system alarmed Germany's neighbours, especially Poland and France.[1]

The annexation of Austria in March 1938 had been carried out by 100,000 German troops who occupied the country within two days. The speed of the operation highlighted the ease with which Germany could transmit huge volumes of military radio traffic without any apparent concern for security.[2]

It has been estimated that by September 1938 there were already around 20,000 Enigma machines in use[3] and by the start of WW2 twelve months later this had increased to some 40,000.[4]

Enigma encipherment was based on the principle of the rotor, as were a number of cipher machines earlier in the century. By adapting it to electrical operation and using a series of internally wired rotors, the substitution of alphabetical characters became automatic.

The Enigma was contained in a portable, lidded box; it had a keyboard with 26 A-Z keys, a lampboard with 26 lamps labelled A-Z, a 'steckerboard' with 26 paired plug sockets, and was powered by an internal battery. The steckerboard allowed cross-plugging between the letter-key circuits, a refinement introduced by the armed services as an improvement on the original commercial model, which had no steckerboard. Most importantly, the Enigma machine contained three electrically wired rotors which were easily installable in any desired order by the operator.

The depression of a keyboard letter-key would light one of the lamps. The illuminated letter represented the encipherment of the keyed letter; its identity would depend upon the exact path taken by the current from the letter key, via the steckerboard, through the internal wiring of each rotor, into and out of a 'reflector rotor' at the left-hand side of the machine, and through the rotors again before finally reaching one particular lamp by way of the steckerboard.

Each of the rotors had 26 positions, A-Z, and these could be set manually by the operator. During operation, each time a key was pressed, the right-hand rotor advanced one position. Every time this rotor completed a revolution, it tripped the centre rotor, advancing it one position. Similarly, each revolution of the centre rotor tripped the left-hand rotor one position. Thus, in use, the rotors advanced in a manner directly comparable to a mechanical revolution counter, such as a car's milometer. By this action the current path through the rotors was therefore changed every time a key was pressed.

A 3-rotor Enigma machine, with lid open, showing stecker-board (with two pairs of steckers in use), keyboard, lampboard and rotors.

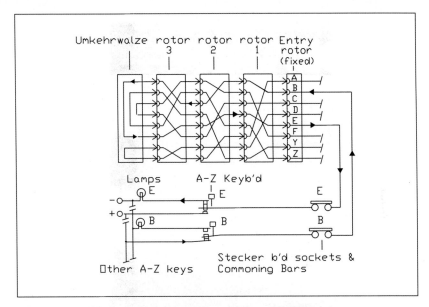

Figure 1: The Enigma rotors (the scrambler).
(For clarity, not all 26 A-Z positions are shown.)

A rotor had a circle of 26 (A–Z) contact studs on its left side and a similar circle of sprung sensing pins on its right side which made contact with the studs of its neighbour, and each rotor had a unique pattern of internal connections between studs and pins. Both the entry commutator (with its 26 contact studs) and the reflector commutator (with its 26 sprung pins) were static, the internal cross-wiring of the latter being of a unique pattern.

The steckerboard, (represented here by only two letter-key positions), consisted of a pair of plug sockets for each letter. Behind the board, a sprung bar normally provided electrical connection between the two. Thus, e.g., the 'B' key circuit was normally connected to the 'B' stud of the entry commutator, etc. However, a cable of two wires, with a two-pin plug at each end, could be plugged into, e.g., the 'B' and 'E' sockets. The insertion of the plugs pushed the sprung bars away from the sockets, and the wires of the cable then connected the upper socket of 'B' to the lower socket of 'E', and the lower socket of 'B' to the upper socket of 'E'. Both entry and exit connections between the two keys were thus now crossed over, creating an additional letter substitution. The number of cables used varied up to twelve.

19

In Figure 1, the closure of letter-key 'B' forms a circuit through the rotors and back via the 'E' line to the 'E' lamp. The letter 'B' has therefore been enciphered to 'E'. The circuit diagram also shows that
a) no letter could be enciphered to itself, and
b) if the state of the machine was such that pressing key 'B' lit lamp 'E', then the reverse was true, i.e. pressing key 'E' would light lamp 'B'. Thus if the encipherment of B were E, the decipherment of E would be B. This allowed the receiver of an enciphered message to decipher that message by keying it into an Enigma, *provided that the receiver's machine was set up identically to that used by the sender.*

Enigma rotors on spindle

Around the periphery of each rotor was a movable ring carrying the indicator letters, A-Z, one of which being visible at any one time through a window in the inner cover of the machine. The ring could be moved round and locked in any one of 26 positions so that the visible indicator letter bore no direct relationship to the position of the wiring in the rotor's core. The position in which the ring was locked relative to the core was called the ring setting. Note that it was an indent on the ring, not on the core, that defined when one rotor would trip its neighbour by one position.

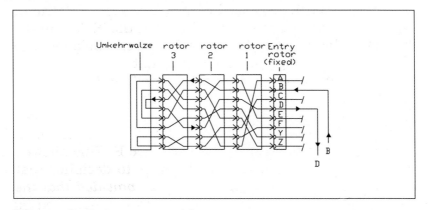

Figure 2: Enigma second key entry.
A second entry of letter 'B' has moved rotor 1 one step (shown as upwards in the figure) and the new rotor circuit results in 'B' being enciphered to 'D'.

With three rotors installed in the machine in any one particular order, there were 26 x 26 x 26 = 17,576 possible rotor states and hence letter substitutions. As the three rotors could be arranged in the machine in any one of six possible sequences there were 6 x 17,576 = 105,456 possible substitutions. With five rotors available, from which three were to be selected, this total was increased ten-fold. The use of the steckerboard increased the permutations still further.

The setting-up procedures of an Enigma varied;[5] prior to the war, settings might be changed according to monthly (or quarterly) and daily lists. These lists were issued to all users within a particular communications network (or keynet). These settings might consist of:

Changed monthly: Rotor order and steckerboard plugging
Changed daily: Ring settings, and initial rotor settings.

In addition, after these settings had been made, the encipher clerk was required to select a message key, say DBY. This would be keyed in twice, producing, say, the encode CHOSTM. The clerk then reset the rotors to DBY, and proceeded to enter the text of the message. Each key stroke lit up one letter on the lampboard; these encoded letters were then transmitted by the wireless operator in Morse code, preceded by CHOSTM.

The receiving de-cipher clerk's Enigma would have had the same initial settings, as he would have been in the same keynet. Therefore, to obtain the clear text he would

a) key in the message key CHOSTM, which would light up DBYDBY

b) set his rotors to DBY

c) key in the enciphered text, which would produce the letters of the original (clear) text one at a time on the lampboard.

— Chapter 3 —

The Polish Codebreakers

In July 1928, the first German wireless messages enciphered by machine were intercepted by Polish monitoring stations. Efforts to decipher them by Captain Maksymilian Ciezki, Director of the Polish Cipher Bureau's German section, were unsuccessful.

In September 1932, Polish mathematicians Marian Rejewski, Jerzy Rozycki and Henryk Zygalski started work as cryptologists at the Polish Cipher Bureau in Warsaw to study the new German machine cipher.[1] During 1931 and 1932 the Bureau had obtained, from a French Intelligence officer Gustave Bertrand, some details of the German military Enigma machine, detailed operating instructions and 'keying' instructions (the initial settings of the machine) used during five months of 1932. It had also obtained an Enigma-enciphered text with its corresponding plain text.[2]

Marian Rejewski was set aside to study the Enigma, and using the information provided he applied his mathematical analysis to the six-letter indicators which started each message. These indicators informed the recipient which rotor settings to use on his machine to allow him to decipher the rest of the message he had received.

From the information provided Rejewski knew that the six-letter groups from messages sent on the same keynet on the same day would, even with different 'message keys', have the same rotor settings. By comparisons he found that certain character link sequences were common in all cases and were logically produced by the six-letter input steps of the first rotor.

An examination of the daily keys for September and October 1932, provided by the French, enabled him to complete his overall analysis by including all key and steckerboard settings. This enabled him to determine the wiring of the first rotor.

He then found that the keys of the September and October messages were of different yearly quarters and that the rotor order had changed between the months. Repeating his analysis he was able to determine the wiring of the now different first rotor. Knowing the wiring of two of the three rotors he was able, by the beginning of 1933, to deduce the wiring of the third rotor and also that of the Umkehrwalze commutator.[3]

The Poles' step-by-step reconstruction of the design of the Enigma eventually made possible the manufacture of working replicas of the machine. During 1933 the Cipher Bureau commissioned the AVA Radio Manufacturing Company of Warsaw to manufacture the components for a number of these replicas.[4]

With the aid of these Enigma replicas the team was frequently able to read German enciphered messages, providing that the keys could be discovered. During 1933 by their study of Enigma messages and by their exploring all possible positions of the rotors the team determined all the elements of the keys.

The cipher team had now begun to solve daily keys, and by using twelve Enigma replicas operated by a team of clerks, they deciphered many Enigma messages. In 1935 their efforts were greatly improved by their invention of the Cyclometer, based on two sets of rotors from their Enigma replicas, and which was manufactured by the AVA Company.[5]

Between 1936 and 1938 the Germans made a number of modifications to their Enigma procedure, and also to the machine detail, thereby so increasing the Polish team's load of analytical work that a more automated process was needed.

In 1938 the team developed the 'Bomba'. This was an electrically driven system of rotors based, essentially, on three pairs of Enigmas.[6] When the keys of three intercepted messages showed linked characteristics, each pair of Enigmas would be set to test the keys of *two* of the three possible combinations. The rotors of all three pairs would be driven through all their 17,576 positions looking for a three-way match and so reveal rotor settings. To reveal the *order* of the rotors Rejewski proposed six Bombas (the Polish plural is 'Bomby') to try all rotor *orders* at the same time. Each machine would stop when it reached a possible solution and the rotor settings tried on an Enigma replica to check whether the key produced plain text.

The three rotors of an Enigma could be placed in the machine in any one of six possible orders; so to analyse all possible orders simultaneously six Bomby were required. Components for these were manufactured by the AVA Company and assembled in secrecy within the Bureau.

Almost simultaneously with the Bomba, Henryk Zygalski developed an alternative way of resolving the message keys. This was a manual method that used a system of 'Perforated Sheets'.[7]

In December 1938 the Germans raised the number of available rotors for each machine to five, from which the operator had to select three for insertion into the machine. By good fortune, though, the lack of a co-ordinated adoption of the additional rotors within the German Services enabled the Bureau team to determine their internal wiring. But the effect of the two additional rotors was to increase the number of Bomby needed for analysis by a factor of ten - from six to sixty, (selecting three from five gives ten possible combinations). Likewise a similar increase in the series of Zygalski 'Perforated Sheets' would be needed.

But at this time the Bureau had other pressing needs, including a demand by their monitoring stations for modern communication equipment, and the need for many more replica Enigmas. The Bureau's limited resources could not cope.[8] As a result the Bureau deci-ded to share its knowledge and experience with its

French and British allies who had the capabilities to build on the Polish success.

In January the French and British met the Poles in Paris but none of the Polish achievements was disclosed. Even by the summer they had not given away any deciphered Wehrmacht messages. Only in July, as war appeared inevitable, was the meeting arranged at which all their information and details of their methods and machinery, including their Cyclometer, Bomba, and 'Perforated Sheets', were made available; they also gave to each ally a copy of the military Enigma machine. In Britain this information arrived at the Government Code & Cipher School at Bletchley Park during August 1939.[9]

— Chapter 4 —

Bletchley Park

The Government Code & Cipher School first encountered Enigma in the mid-1930s when noting increased Italian naval activity in the Mediterranean during the Italian invasion of Abyssinia. From intercepted messages they realised that the Italians had started using a cipher machine, soon recognised as the early, commercial, Enigma. GCCS was by then familiar with the details of this simpler version which lacked the steckerboard of the military Enigma. They were able to solve many daily keys but, unlike the Polish Cipher Bureau, had no mathematicians working on the problem and were using the so-called 'Rod' method that involved wooden rods on which paper strips, with the cipher letters of each rotor, were stuck. They had, however, failed to resolve the military Enigma equipped with the steckerboard.[1]

During September 1939 a recently formed team of mathematicians, including Peter Twinn and Alan Turing, were already working on resolving this Enigma and the development of a Bombe. John Jeffreys was committed to the construction of the increased number of sets of Zygalski perforated sheets needed to continue reading the current Enigma messages using the Polish method.[1]

John Jeffreys had completed the 60 sets of perforated sheets by the beginning of 1940 and these became the sole means of deciphering the Enigma transmissions that were being intercepted by radio listening-posts now set up in locations around the country. However, the use of these perforated sheets was dependent on the Polish method of attacking the enciphered text by concentrating on the six-letter group known to represent the three-letter message key typed in twice (see page 21). Their usefulness therefore depended entirely upon the Germans' continuing to incorporate this repetition in their procedure - which in fact was not to continue for very many more months.

During this time Alan Turing discarded the Polish Bomba, based on six sets of Enigma rotors coupled together, designed to exploit the weakness inherent in the repeated encipherment of the three-letter key. He envisaged a different approach for his Bombe that would result in a far more powerful machine.

Turing concentrated on the looser, more-embracing 'probable word' method* for breaking the Enigma; this involved matching a plain text word or phrase, thought likely to be present in a certain position of the original Enigma message, to a relevant portion of the cipher text. He would study combinations of letter pairings between the two groups of letters, which formed a closed loop or loops of related letter pairs, and then check whether such a loop or loops could be produced by any combination of rotor settings of the 60 possible rotor orders. If so, the probable word and its encipherment might be validated, and the rotor settings and steckered letters responsible might be applied to a checking machine, simulating an Enigma machine. If the check proved valid, the complete Enigma message text might be entered to obtain the original clear text.[1]

To achieve this he required a larger array of scramblers to represent the letter pairings making up the 'closed loops'. The scramblers would need to have separate input and output channels to allow interconnected circuits through them according to the sequence of letter pairings within a loop. He introduced a 26-position register to evaluate the outcome of the loop tests at each successive combination of rotor positions. Finally a high-speed machine would be needed to perform the automatic search of all the rotor positions of the scramblers in a short time.

Converting this proposed design into a practical machine was the engineering problem to be presented to The British Tabulating Machine Company (BTM) and Harold Keen.

---

* See Appendix 1.

BTM became involved with the Bletchley Park (BP) operation during the autumn of 1939 when Commander Edward Travis, at that time the Deputy Director of GCCS, visited Letchworth to discuss the design and manufacture of the Turing Bombe. The discussion took place with the Managing Director, Mr Bailey, and Harold Keen, and resulted in a contract code-named 'CANTAB'.[2]

There thus began a close association between BTM and BP from the autumn of 1939. During the ensuing months and years the increasing success of the project required continuous development, and the ever-widening employment of the Bombe would commit BTM to the allocation of a considerable proportion of its resources to an increasing production. The enormously successful application of the Bombe by BP would result in an ever-growing staff of codebreakers and supporting staff which had begun with several hundred at the beginning of 1940 and would grow to several thousand by 1945. Reciprocal liaison teams were constant visitors to both BTM and BP and continued the close co-operation until the end of the European war in May 1945. During this time the Bombe was developed to counter German modifications to the Enigma and to its usage procedure, and to meet increasing demands from BP. Four prototype machines were built and installed by the summer of 1940; production followed quickly in 1941 and was considerably increased from 1942. Installation teams were formed by BTM and efficient maintenance was organised for the various Bombe sites that were set up in close proximity to BP. By the end of the European War around two hundred machines had been manufactured and installed at various sites, and nearly two thousand operators, including over seventeen hundred WRNS personnel, were employed.

— Chapter 5 —

Doc Keen and CANTAB

There is no detailed record of the meetings which took place between Alan Turing, with his associates, and Harold Keen during the period immediately following the CANTAB agreement, but a successful outcome of these meetings, and of the close collaboration between the two sides, became apparent by the beginning of 1940.

At BTM Doc Keen pursued his design in his Engineering Department which combined a design office, an engineering team and experimental workshop facilities. Later he was to be supported by the company's manufacturing facility which was by that time engaged with increasing production commitments with punched card equipment in addition to the manufacture of aircraft parts for the general war effort.

From being the original code-name for the projected design and manufacture of the Bombe, the eventual machine became known within the company generally as the CANTAB machine, except by those who were directly involved and knew its true purpose.

The Bletchley Park team gained from the knowledge of the Polish successes, the mechanisms employed, and the Zygalski sheets which Jeffreys was rapidly bringing into use. They were developing their own version of the Bombe but as the war had already started there was short time to bring the proposed machine into service, and the interim use of the only alternative, the perforated sheets, was slow and laborious.

The urgent need for the Bombe became clear on the 10 May 1940, the day of the invasion of France, when the Germans suddenly changed the Enigma operating procedures. From this date, enciphering clerks only had to type in the message key once, not twice as hitherto. This change at once made the perforated sheets useless. From then until the Bombe prototypes became available to make use of 'cribs', the breaking of Enigma messages relied on a number of intelligent guesses based upon bad Enigma operator habits - this was a craft that BP had by then been rapidly developing.

In late 1939 Doc Keen, to meet the urgency of the situation, had restricted new and unproven designs to a minimum and adapted, as far as possible, suitable and proven components already being manufactured in quantity for BTM's own products. This approach, coupled with a close-knit design, manufacture and assembly operation was to take place within the security of his own department, and would produce the prototypes in the shortest possible time.

The basic principle behind all BTM equipment was the recording of numerical and alphabetical information by means of accurately punched holes in Hollerith cards. The Hollerith card was around $7^1/_2$ x $3^1/_2$ inches in size with a capacity of eighty vertical columns, each able to hold an alphabetical or numerical character, the value of which was represented by the vertical position of a hole, or holes, punched therein. By this means specified groups, or 'fields', of card columns, would typically hold information data while other columns held the category, or type, of the information data. In other equipment, operating in repeated mechanical cycles, the holes punched would subsequently be sensed by small metal brushes thus allowing timed, electrical, clock-pulses of current to pass through. Electro-mechanisms were activated via the punched cards; for example card sorters that could automatically extract from a batch of cards those holding specific types of data etc., or could sort cards into numerical or alphabetical order. Numerical and £sd accumulators and printing mechanisms were also similarly controlled. Timed electrical clock pulses were distributed within or between mechanisms by means of commutators with circular rows of contact segments and rotating sensing brushes.

This particular technology, coupled with the company's expertise with the use of electromagnetic relays as a means of control, or as switches, was well suited to a speedy solution of CANTAB. The kernel of the design was the scrambler and its three rotors.

The CANTAB scrambler, unlike the Enigma scrambler, needed to be double-ended (to provide separate input and output access) to enable continuous circuits through several scramblers coupled together in series and in either direction. There also had to be clear access to individual rotors for their easy removal and replacement by an operator when the rotor order within a scrambler needed to be changed during use.

A theoretical double-ended scrambler

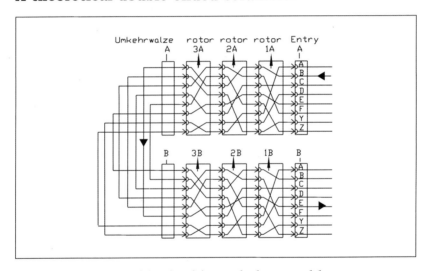

Figure 3: A possible double-ended scrambler.
(Based on the Enigma scrambler – see Figures 1 and 2.)

Each rotor has **two** circular rows of contact studs and brushes 1A, 2A, 3A, and 1B, 2B, 3B with identical wiring. The entry commutator has two rows of contact studs, A and B, and the *Umkehrwalze* has two rows of brushes. The return paths from the *Umkehrwalze* brushes of Row 'A' are diverted to *Umkehrwalze* Row 'B' so that the return paths are now through the duplicate set of rotor circuits.

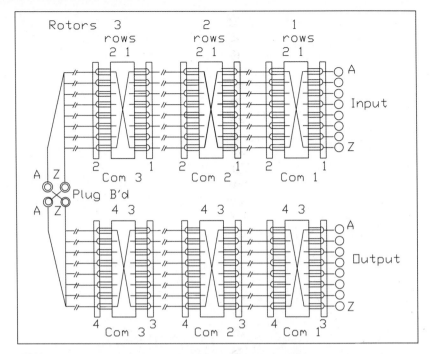

Figure 4 (above): The CANTAB scrambler.
Each rotor, e.g. rotor 1, has four rows of sensing brushes, with cross-wiring between rows 1 and 2, and between rows 3 and 4, which make contact with corresponding rows of segments 1 and 2, and 3 and 4, of commutator 1.
Note 1: Connections shown as ——//—— are external between the three fixed commutators.
Note 2: The 26-way Input and Output are connected to 26-way jacks.

Figure 5 (p 34, top): The scrambler drive mechanism.
Two positions of the upper row of scramblers are shown; drive shafts provide continuous drive to the top rotors and the carry mechanisms of the lower rows. The left-hand position shows the commutators, fixed to a backplate, and each has four circular rows of contact segments. In the right-hand position the commutators are removed to show the rotor drive mechanisms. The rotor shafts protrude to the front.

Each top rotor shaft is driven via worm gears and a ratchet-wheel/drive-pawl coupling. Each lower rotor shaft is moved through a single step by the reciprocal motion of a common 'carry bar', extending along each row, and via a ratchet-wheel/drive-pawl coupling. The energising of a solenoid will start the movement of a carry bar by its armature moving the hooked lever of the carry bar into engagement with

33

the cam-operated drive-pawl.

A rotor engages with its shaft by means of a mating key and keyway, and when locked the sensing brushes are pressured against the commutator.

Note 1. The ratchet-wheel/drive-pawl mechanisms allow a rotor shaft and ratchet-wheel to turn clockwise past the drive-pawl. Thus a mounted rotor may be turned manually to any A-Z position according to a Bombe test Menu.

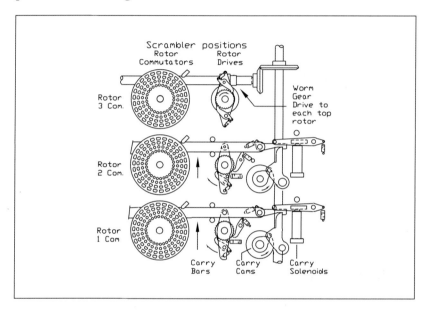

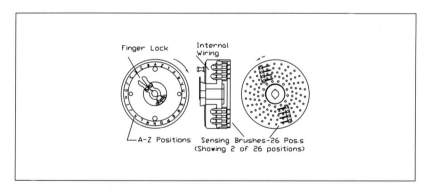

Figure 6 (lower): The rotor.
The left-hand (front) view shows the finger lock which, by locating in a shaft groove, holds the rotor to its shaft. The right-hand (rear) view shows two of the twenty-six groups of four sensing brushes.

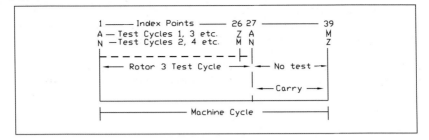

Figure 7: The 3-rotor Bombe test cycle.

The test cycle of rotor 3 starts at index point 1 and completes a revolution by index point 26. A test pulse is fed to one A-Z position of rotor 1 entry commutator at every index point as rotor 3 sensing brushes pass over successive commutator segments.

At index point 27 the test cycle is complete and a carry solenoid is energised to start a carry action to rotor 2 during the last 13 index points. Rotor 3 continues to turn but no test occurs, and by the index point 39 it has turned through a further 13 positions. At the start of the next machine cycle, if the rotor is in position 14 (letter 'N'), the next test cycle will finish at 'M'.

Each alternate test cycle of rotor 3 will start at either 'A' or 'N'; this is immaterial as all A-Z positions are tested during the test cycle.

The Speed of the 3-Rotor Bombe

To ensure maximum reliability of the new machine the overall speed was selected to provide generous timing margins. On the earlier Bombes the sensing rate of commutator segments was 20 to 25 per second. As a general indication of overall performance level the following calculation uses a sensing rate of 20 per second.

Time for sensing all 26 segments of a commutator = 1.3 sec.
Time between segments (index points) = 0.05 sec.
Carry time (13 index points) = 0.65 secs, and a machine cycle (rotor test cycle + carry) = 1.95 secs.

So, to test all positions of 3 rotors takes 1.95 secs x 26 x 26 = 22 mins, and to test all six different orders of 3 rotors takes 132 mins. Finally, to test all combinations of 3 from 5 rotors takes 132 mins x 10 = 22 hours (ignoring any interim successful test result, and the additional time to change the rotor orders when required).

Later models were continuously improved, and the indicated 22-hour test time probably reduced to a figure closer to 15 hours.

Standard BTM units and components were employed to provide the various functions. Clutch units were adapted to control the main machine cycle, the drive to the rotors and the carry mechanism, and BTM cam-operated contacts were used to provide the timing pulses generated during the machine cycle. Sensing brushes were employed by the thousand in the rotors, and the established technique in the use of commutators was critical. Standard Hollerith plugboards were used to provide the unique *Umkehrwalze* interconnections.

Initially Siemens high-speed relays were used to sense the rotor test circuits. To provide a visual indicator of the state of the Turing Register after the event of a successful 'Stop', a standard BTM indicator-unit was used.

The flexibility in the design of providing pluggable connections where possible allowed for future changes and developments. An immediate example occurred during the design stage when Gordon Welchman introduced his 'diagonal board' where the use of multiple connectors allowed easy linking to his unit. Again, if the Germans had ever introduced new *Umkehrwalze* wiring, the BTM plug boards would have enabled simple alteration by re-plugging instead of re-wiring each Bombe.

Turing's concept required a considerable number of scramblers for testing cribs of varying lengths and testing the multiple closed loops. At one early meeting held at the White Hart Inn in Buckingham, Peter Twinn mentioned to Doc Keen that the eventual need could be for a machine with a configuration of up to forty scramblers.[1] A compromise was reached limiting the number to ten in the first two prototypes in order to satisfy the Turing requirement of three 3-scrambler groups, and at the same time to prove the engineering design. In the two following prototypes with the diagonal board the number was increased to twelve to allow additional 2-scrambler 'links' of letter pairs as required by Gordon Welchman. However, by the end of 1941 Doc Keen was producing Bombes having three rows of twelve scramblers, to provide thirty-six in total, and so the original prediction of 1939 was approaching reality.

By the beginning of 1940 the main mechanical design was established and manufacture of the prototypes had started.[2]

Gordon Welchman, who also was a mathematician, and who had joined BP in September 1939, soon became involved in the development of the Bombe. Within three months he had proposed his diagonal board, a means by which the Bombe scramblers could be interconnected in a more extended manner compared to Turing's original conception. By taking advantage of the reciprocal steckering nature of the Enigma steckerboard plugging, more letter-pairings could be used in association with Turing's closed loops and would provide much stronger test criteria from a shorter portion of a crib by requiring fewer closed loops. Its effect was to drastically reduce the number of *doubtful* test solutions and so greatly reduce the number of Bombe runs that would be needed. The importance of the diagonal board required its immediate adoption into the Bombe design.[3]

The manufacture of two prototypes to the original Turing design was in progress at the start of 1940 but immediate modifications were made to incorporate the diagonal board into the design, and the manufacture of two further prototypes was begun.

By the spring of 1940 an early trial machine was available for BP to carry out initial tests. By the early summer of 1940, and after modifications resulting from the preliminary trials, two Turing prototypes were installed at Bletchley Park; these were followed after a short interval by the two prototypes of Welchman's

Bombe which was to become the basic pattern for future machines.

— Chapter 6 —

The Bombe Makers

After the necessary trials at BP the two Welchman prototypes were cleared for production. By the summer of 1941, the first enlarged production models arrived.[1] Their whole structure had been redesigned to accommodate the additional scramblers and drives. A final design with three banks, each of twelve scramblers, was settled on and the complete design rationalised.

The original prototype, being limited to twelve scramblers, would cater for a menu to test closed loops plus several associated links of letter pairs. The final version, having thirty-six scramblers, now had the facility for several separate or combined tests. The facility for up to three such tests was provided, with separate test registers and diagonal boards. The complete flexibility that enabled interconnection between the 36 scramblers, diagonal boards and registers required an array of up to 230 26-way jacks and batches of 26-way plug-in cable connectors. Each scrambler to be used in a test run needed a complement of the 5 uniquely wired rotors. Therefore each Bombe required a total of 180 rotors.

By the summer of 1941 there were 4 to 6 Bombes at BP, installed in the then Hut 11, and a similar number in some converted stables at Adstock Manor in the village of Adstock, with a 'Bombe Hut' being built in Wavendon village at Wavendon House.[2] Delivery of these machines was by ordinary, unobtrusive, covered lorries, the normal method used for delivering BTM's own machines and which attracted no undue attention.

Eventually these three sites had between them some 24 to 30 Bombes. Gayhurst Manor was requisitioned and prepared to accommodate 16 more machines. By the time these were installed the overall total had reached between 40 to 46, and an eventual total of 70 was assumed.

For this number of machines accommodation for 700 operators, WRNS personnel, became necessary.[2]

The 3-rotor Bombe ATLANTA was one of ten in the American bay at Eastcote, 1943-5, each named after an American city. This front view shows the 36 scramblers and three indicator rotors. The right-hand side panel, shown open, holds the A-Z input-letter switches. The Umkehrwalze plugboard is mounted on the left-hand side-panel. *(NARA photo no. 457 - Ent 9032 - Ex1426 - 524160 - 9/1)*

Rear view of the 3-rotor Bombe ATLANTA, showing the nine columns of 26-way jacks for connection between scramblers, diagonal boards and Registers, connections being made by pluggable cable connectors. In the right-hand background, can be seen a storage rack for the many rotors.

(NARA photo no. 457 - Ent 9032 - Ex1426 - 524160 - 9/4)

Gayhurst Manor itself was to accommodate several hundred.

By 1942 BTM were producing Bombes in batches of six and each was taking just six weeks to build.[2]

From 1939 the output of BTM's own punched-card machines was taken for use by Government departments and by the armed services, and even its own Customer Service Bureaux were working for the Government.

Later a small installation of BTM punched-card machines was set up at BP in Hut 7 to provide the means for the rapid recording and accessing of the quantities of deciphered Enigma data needed for future reference; this installation was rapidly enlarged, eventually requiring an operating staff of several hundred.

During this time BTM was, in addition, producing aircraft parts, such as bomb-sights, as its contribution to the general war effort. By 1943 its work force probably doubled and production output was vastly increased.

During 1942 there was a general increase in war activity on the fronts in Egypt and Russia, and from the later Allied landings in Algeria and Morocco. This resulted in a large increase in German military communications and in the volume of Enigma traffic.[3] At BP this caused an increase in its deciphering activity which highlighted a current shortage of Bombes. The need for well in excess of the planned 70 Bombes was realised. New Admiralty orders were placed with BTM and production greatly expanded.

Priority was now given to the supply of materials, although during late 1942 and early 1943 a shortage of raw materials required urgent action and Admiralty pressure on various suppliers and Government departments became necessary.[4]

A large support operation was brought into being within the company to provide the myriad components required. A second manufacturing plant was set up to produce mechanical components at the pre-war Ascot Training Centre in Letchworth, and was completely furnished with machine tools by the government.

For the supply of less sensitive items the local Spirella factory, which in peacetime had produced corsets, and in 1940 had diverted to parachutes, was now partly occupied to undertake the assembly of the uniquely wired rotors by several hundred staff during day and night shifts. In addition, a number of subcontractors in the locality were engaged to make other parts not needing machine tools, and to assemble the miles of electrical cables.

The problem of housing the increased numbers of Bombes was solved by using newly constructed buildings at Stanmore by August 1942 and the accommodation for the large number of WRNS personnel was found nearby. During 1943 some 20 Bombes had been installed there. The Stanmore establishment was quickly repeated at Eastcote in West London and accommodation for 800 WRNS personnel provided in a new building. These two establishments eventually housed the main bulk of machines, those housed at the original sites at Adstock and Wavendon being transferred. At BP only a few were retained for training and demonstration.[5] By March 1943 sixty Bombes had been installed, and by the end of the European War there were in excess of 200.

With the increased production came the need for enlarged installation teams. There also arose a need to form engineering teams for on-site overhauls of machines already in heavy use. These teams were in addition to those of the site maintenance organisation.

The site maintenance was controlled by RAF Sergeant Jones; one of the original BTM engineers, he was eventually made responsible for the overall maintenance of all machines wherever situated.

RAF engineers formed the major part of the maintenance organisation. One member of this organisation was Peter Howkins. He recalls

'My first involvement with the code-breaking project was being told to attend an interview at the Air Ministry in Whitehall, around August 1942. I think the interview was with a Squadron Leader Jones. He may have previously worked for BTM, but he seemed to be in charge of the engineering maintenance side of the project.

I had been in the RAF some two years before the interview, having completed two aircraft electrical courses and spending some time with a Fighter Squadron. I had no previous involvement with BTM. As a result of the interview a posting came through about three months later, instructing me to report to RAF Chicksands (Priory), near Shefford, Beds. From there, after about three days, I was taken to Stanmore and introduced to a Flight Sergeant Eric Dyson, who was running the station and, I think, had been an employee of BTM. The delay between the first interview and arriving at Stanmore was, I now know, due to security clearance.

When I started at Stanmore the section was comparatively small, there being some fifty or so RAF people. This number built up to at least eighty or more. To my knowledge only a handful had previous BTM employment. There were at least three hundred WRNS, and a few GPO civilians working on their own equipment; no Americans or WRAF people worked at Stanmore.

As a matter of interest, all the RAF personnel when I first arrived were billeted out in private homes around Stanmore. Later we were 'bussed' to the outstation at Eastcote for 'bed and breakfast'. Eventually sleeping accommodation was built for us at Stanmore and we had our meals in part of the WRNS mess.

The maintenance set-up was roughly one RAF technician to two bays, (each) consisting of approximately 16 - 20 Bombes. A small back-up engineering group and a small workshop that was equipped for making, repairing and redesigning machine parts. Incidentally there were several WRNS who worked on the engineering maintenance side.

In my opinion the 3-wheel Bombes were very reliable considering they were expected to run 24 hours a day, 7 days a week. I am sure the only 3-wheel versions at Stanmore were those with three banks of twelve by three drums, plus four indicator drums. I think only about eight machines had typewriter outputs and, I'm pretty sure, no electric typewriters were ever fitted at Stanmore. Each bay had a checking machine which, I assume, was made by BTM*, these were used to prove a 'STOP', to ensure that it had not been caused by a machine or plugging fault. Sometimes a machine would miss a legal 'STOP'; the Bletchley people would know this when the code was eventually broken and then there would be a great inquiry as to why it had happened.

There were a number of common problems which had to be dealt with, one of these being the wear of the top commutators (fast drives). The wear meant removing the three commutators of that particular bank and replacing them with a new set which usually had the one commutator replaced by soldering the connections on the back. This procedure was quite time-consuming. One of my first jobs was to unsolder the top commutator and solder a replacement back on - one sort of 'graduated' out of that job.

The small workshop made great efforts to produce a spring-loaded top com., which was quite ambi-tious; they even made an automatic spring-making machine. This, of course, would save a tremendous amount of time just to be able to unscrew the worn com. and fit a new one. I think there were problems with these springs making good contact and I cannot remember whether they were put into general use.

The brushes on each drum were supposed to be inspected before being clipped into position - so long as this was done conscientiously I do not remember brushes being a major problem.

The 26-way plugs used on the rear of the machine for plugging up the 'MENU' were always going 'open circuit' due to the girls unplugging them by pulling the wires instead of the plug itself. A gadget was finally

---

* These checking units were manufactured by BTM with rotors used by Bombe scramblers. Later versions of the rotors used in these units were fitted with sensing fingers in place of sensing brushes. These allowed an operator to hand-turn the rotors in either direction when setting up to test a 'Stop'.

designed to test for 'open circuits' before the plugs were used

There were over a hundred Bombes, some 16 to 20 to a bay and operated on a three 'watch' system. Each bay was named after a country or city of the British Empire and a resident technician looked after the day-to-day engineering problems and carried out the planned maintenance for each Bombe.

A small engineering back-up group of ten to twelve people (of which I was one) had the task of dealing with major problems, such as changing main clutches, replacing carry bars and mechanisms - the drum drive shafts. This type of fault could result in the Bombe being out of action for quite a number of hours, which did not please the people at Bletchley. We were also called in if a fault could not be found within a reasonable time by the bay technician. On odd occasions people from Letchworth were called in if necessary.

I think the majority of the 3-wheel Bombes were there when I arrived, but it was not long before the 4-wheel versions arrived at intervals of, perhaps, three or four weeks or longer. These were a headache, with the electronics and the 4th wheel drive (i.e. the high-speed 4th rotors) being the main problems. They probably needed quite a lot more development time, which was not an option in those days. When the war was obviously coming to an end, the delivery of machines seemed to speed up and virtually came in one door and went out of another for scrapping.

The whole building was nearly blown up by a flying-bomb, which exploded three hundred yards away. It damaged the perimeter wall and a couple of bays.

Generally speaking, the outstation was well run with a lot of enthusiasm and dedication which, by all accounts, was very successful. If a 'STOP' was sent to Bletchley, and which ultimately broke the code there would be an announcement by the WRNS officer in charge of the watch and the whole place would erupt.

When the war in Europe finally finished I was sent to Bletchley Park and worked at Drayton Parslow. Because of that I did not see any of the scrapping or clearing of the buildings at Stanmore.'

Installation sites

Early machines were installed at BP, Adstock and Wavendon House and together there were between 24 and 30. Sites were then created at Crawley Grange and Gayhurst manor By 1943 at London Road, Stanmore there were about 20, and at Eastcote there were a similar number.

By the middle of 1942 there was a major increase in demand. New orders were placed with BTM and priorities were given to the supply of materials. Eventually the Stanmore and Eastcote sites were expanded, taking Bombes from Wavendon and Adstock. And accommodation for 800-900 WRNS operators was provided.

David Whitehead[6] recalls the activity at Eastcote during late 1943-4

'In a Bombe Bay there would be up to a dozen Bombes or more. The many rotors for use on the Bombes were kept on a large rack, each unique rotor type identified by colour coding.

Operation of each machine required an optimum of two Wrens. A new 'job' for a test run came as a 'Menu' from Hut 6 at Bletchley Park as a result of examining a likely crib in an Enigma encrypted message. The resultant 'links' found would be the basis for such detail as, for example, the selection of scramblers to be used, interconnections between them, the type of rotors to be fitted and the setting of each rotor. One operator would carry out the scrambler interconnection plugging at the rear of the Bombe while the other would select the correct rotors, examine them for any defects and fit them to the scramblers, turning each to the required letter on the Menu.

When the setting-up was complete both operators would double-check before starting the test run. When a 'Stop' occurred the letter registered on the check unit and the positions of the indicator rotors were noted. These details were rushed to the Checking Room where a Wren would set up a machine (sometimes called the Letchworth Enigma*); it consisted essentially of a Bombe scrambler, hand operated and electrically powered accordingly. Starting with the first 'input' letter she would follow the menu links, altering the rotors accordingly. If the 'Stop' was a good one she would arrive back at the beginning of the menu with the same letter as the input. On the way perhaps she would have turned up some confirmations of some steckered character pairs (e.g. M steckered to H), as well as some 'self-steckers' such as F steckered to itself. More often than not though there were also some contradictions (M appearing as steckered to H, but at the same time H steckered to W). If it was an exceptionally good 'Stop' there would be many confirmations and self-steckers with no contradictions, and this would immediately be transmitted to BP.'

The early Bombes were operated by RAF and army personnel. In 1941, however, the Women's Royal Naval Service would take over. From that time the number of WRNS operators would eventually rise to nearly eighteen hundred.

At BP, Harold Fletcher who, with Malcolm Saunders, was controlling the Bombe programme, felt there might be a danger of loss of morale and a drop in efficiency and so devised a talk to give an insight into the general purpose of the machines. These talks involved all the WRNS who had already arrived. He repeated these talks to new WRNS, the RAF maintenance engineers and also to US Army personnel who were operating a number of Bombes at Eastcote. He and Malcolm Saunders were also active in boosting the morale of factory workers in the Letchworth area who were involved with the manufacture of Bombe components.[7]

In order to continue this general morale-building exercise it was probably Harold Fletcher who also organised the visits to BTM at Letchworth for batches of WRNS from Stanmore and Eastcote, there to see their Bombes being manufactured. It is also probable that the

---

* Built at BTM, Letchworth. See also Hinsley & Stripp, p116.

quite regular appearance of WRNS was a welcome experience to the Bombe-makers. Many of the WRNS who visited BTM wrote afterwards to Doc Keen, including many from the Stanmore unit during 1943 and 1944.* Typical of these letters is one written by Petty Officer Ruth Harris, at the WRNS Quarters, Canons Corner, Stanmore, and dated 19th March 1943. She writes

Dear Dr. Keen,
   We all feel we should like to try and express some of very real admiration we feel for all those working at Hollerith. And also our gratitude for being allowed to go round the factory. It was all intensely interesting, and we would like to have spent days and days there instead of a few hours. I am sure that none of us will ever forget our visit to Letchworth. Not the least impressive thing we found was the extra-ordinary spirit of co-operation throughout the firm.

   We feel most indebted to you personally for so very kindly giving up so much of your valuable time to us . . . we appreciate it all more than we can say.

Another letter came from Chief Petty Officer Pamela Walker, dated 5th April 1943

   . . . we all had a marvellous day on Thursday, we thoroughly enjoyed it and we so appreciated the way in which you all gave up your precious time to show us around.
   Although we have always appreciated the finished article, I am quite certain that it will be ten times more appreciated now that we have seen all that goes on behind it.
   Of one thing I am quite certain and that is that none of the people who have been round the works will ever criticise your production - we all thought it was really

* A number of such letters are in the possession of the author.

wonderful - and the hours that your people put in - made us feel rather ashamed of ourselves . . .*

At the end of 1942 a US Army contingent was sent to BP. Its three units - 6811th, 6812th and 6813th Signal Security Detachments - dealt with interception, Bombes and cryptanalysis. The 6812th with 200 men under Captain Mortimer Stewart, a Texan and former IBM employee, worked first at Stanmore and then at Ruislip.** Its work area was called UNITED STATES and each of its 12 Bombes was named after a US city. The Americans were pleased to be working with the WRNS. One amazed lieutenant noted that the buildings at Stanmore 'contained marvellous machines and many attractive ladies. The machines were made by the British Tabulating Machine Company, and the ladies by God.' [8]

---

* Other Wrens at Stanmore who wrote to Doc Keen after visiting BTM were Norma Baker, Jeanne Bisgood, Jon Etherington, Rachel S Hubbh, Una Jey, Morag Maclennan, Valerie Nurse, Brenda Peat, Isabel M C Smyth, Betty Swan, and Vivien Williams, and also Jillian Vrang of Crawley Grange.

** The US contingent actually lived in a tented encampment in Ruislip Woods (Ref: West. *GCHQ*. p240). They were working at the Eastcote site from 1st February 1944 to 7th May 1945 in the United States bay.

— Chapter 7 —

The Fourth Rotor

By the middle of 1941 Bletchley Park's Bombes were primarily being used for breaking German Army and Air Force keys; the U-boat Enigma was not being broken. German surface vessels and coastal-water traffic were using the 'Home Waters' key - which could be broken but did not give details of U-boat activities in the Atlantic.[1]

BP had, during 1941, obtained the German 'Short Weather Cipher', and also the Kriegsmarine's weather cipher, from listening to weather ships' reports. Eventually BP could read the plain texts of the U-boat weather reports and these served as 'cribs'.[2]

By May 1941 BP was reading these Enigma messages and as a result there were successful sinkings of enemy surface ships in the Atlantic. These successes caused German concerns about security and resulted in changes in Enigma usage procedures, and by October U-boat High Command communications started using a new TRITON 'keynet', and this was followed by a number of others.[3]

At the beginning of 1942 the German Navy, in an effort to improve security, introduced a special narrow, manually settable, rotor, called 'Beta', fitted to the Enigma between the third rotor and a new, narrow, *Umkehrwalze*. They called this modified version of the Enigma machine the 'M4', and it went into service on the U-boat TRITON keynet.

Its introduction multiplied the number of possible test cycles for a Bombe by a factor of twenty-six. BP, nevertheless, had gained the knowledge of the rotor wiring and this enabled them to solve three TRITON keys, but each of those were solved only by the use of six three-rotor Bombes taking seventeen days for the work.[4]

The urgent need came for a fourth rotor, similarly positioned within each scrambler of the Bombe. In addition to the particular wiring it also needed to turn at high speed to minimise the potential 26-times longer test time necessitated by the additional rotor.

The task of developing the new Bombe rotor was given to C.E. Wynn-Williams of the Telecommunications Research Establishment at Malvern, in association with A.J. Parsons, a design engineer at Mawdsleys of Dursley. It was clear that high-speed sensing of 'stops' would necessitate electronic methods in place of the relatively slow electro-mechanical relays employed in the 3-wheel Bombes.[5] The essential need was to perfect a reliable, heavy-usage, commutator with high-speed sensing. The system adopted was broadly similar to the armature and carbon brushes used in conventional electric motors, and employed 26 narrow copper segments imbedded in the periphery of a commutator and sensed by 26 narrow carbon brushes.

An experimental sensing and display unit was made at Malvern. The development of a working prototype suitable for small-quantity production was allocated to a group at the Post Office Engineering Research Station, Dollis Hill, London, under the direction of T.H. Flowers (later Dr 'Tommy' Flowers, of 'Colossus' fame).

Development started in the spring of 1942 and it was the end of 1943 before the problems encountered could be resolved and the 12 sets of equipment for Eastcote put into production.[5]

The Keen Machine (The BTM 4-rotor Bombe)

During 1942 Doc Keen initially attempted to provide a quick solution, however temporary, with four Bombes linked together and called 'The Giant'; this was unsuccessful and he started developing his existing Bombe design to include the fourth rotors. He had already improved the carry mechanism of the 3-rotor Bombe making it faster in action, and experience gained from the many 3-rotor Bombes in service had also shown that he could considerably reduce the margin of safety originally allowed for in the duration of sensing brush to segment contact, and of the test pulse.

He continued using high-speed relays and therefore the maximum 'High speed' that could be used for the fourth rotor was restricted by their use. Finally, he introduced gas-filled valves to generate the precise test-pulses required.

Eventually the incorporation of the fourth rotor coupling to a 3-rotor Bombe and the timing arrangements involved were similar in principle to both the Keen machine and the Cobra. It was required to connect the circuitry of the fourth rotor in the same position relative to that of the three rotors as in the Enigma machine, between the rotor-3 outlet and the *Umkehrwalze* commutator. On the Keen machine, this allowed the 36 fourth rotors, and their high-speed drives, to be physically grouped together in an extension of the Bombe mainframe, separate from the 36 standard scramblers, yet synchronised with them. In this manner the existing 36-scrambler arrangement was largely undisturbed.

The synchronisation between the two rotor drives was possibly achieved by a mechanical linkage. The generation of electronic test pulses and their synchronisation with the rotor drives was an additional problem.[6]

During July 1943 the Germans introduced a second, alternative, fourth rotor, the 'Gamma'. The selection of this second rotor during a Bombe test run required that the two now had to be interchangeable. The total suite of rotors for selection had now increased to nine.

In order to obtain the maximum speed of the fourth rotor commensurate with his sensing relays Doc Keen
a)   selected a maximum high-speed that still provided the length of test pulses required[6] and
b)   reduced the speed of rotor-3 to provide sufficient brush-to-segment contact duration within each Index point to cover the resulting rotor-4 test cycle time. A deceleration/acceleration cam was also included in the drive of each rotor. This provided a lower speed during

the brush sensing which increased its duration without reducing the overall rotor speed; the deceleration was immediately followed by the (compensating) accelerated speed for the remainder of the index point.

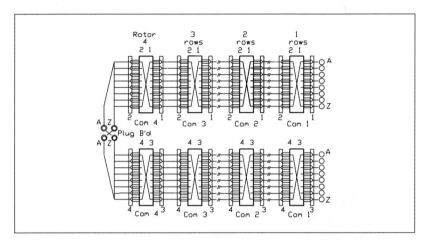

Figure 8: A 4-rotor scrambler (in principle[6]).
a) The fourth rotor is shown located between rotor-3 and the *Umkehrwalze*.
b) The fourth rotor, selected from two, is interchangeable.

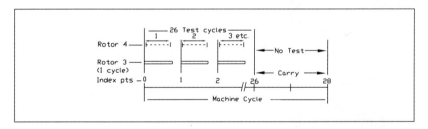

Figure 9: General timings of the 4-rotor Bombe.
The rate of the sensing pulses entering rotor-1 is now related to the high-speed fourth rotor and the sensing of its 26 segments. A complete test cycle of rotor-4 occurs within each of the 26 index points of rotor-3, during the brush/segment contact. So one sensing cycle of rotor-3 achieves the sensing of all positions of both rotors 3 and 4. This sequence is repeated for each position of rotors 2 and 1 as they are stepped round by carry actions. So the time to test one order of four rotors remains a function of (Time to test rotor-3) x 26 x 26, just as for the 3-rotor machine. (But the *real* time will be affected by the *actual speed* of rotor-3.)

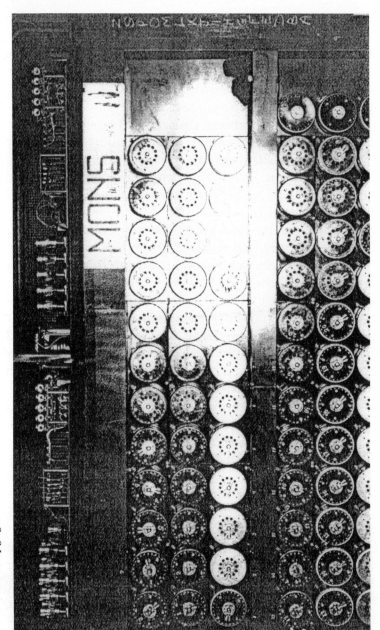

The Bombe MONS is believed to be one of eight 4-rotor bombes in the Belgian bay at Eastcote, 1943-5. Above the 'standard' 3-rotor assemblies are two groups of 5 valve-pairs and components believed to be part of a high-speed pulse generator circuit (see Note 6 to Chapter 7).

(Photo reproduced with the permission of the Controller of HMSO).

The 4-rotor Bombe performance

The performance levels of the 3-rotor Bombe at various stages of development are not accurately defined, although an accepted minimum may be based on the sensing rate of 20-25 pulses per second for rotor-3. During later development the rotor-3 speed was increased and the faster carry action allowed a shorter machine cycle of 30 index points.

The version having a reduced machine cycle appeared by 1943 and might have increased the performance level by up to 30%.

For the 4-rotor Bombe, assessment of the 'Very High Speed' of the fourth rotor relies upon the recollections of informed engineers who were associated with development or installation of the machines. This situation would apply to the BTM 4-rotor Bombe, where a speed range based upon 1000+ rpm has been estimated and supported by recorded detail of 1944,[6] and also to the Cobra for which a final speed of 1200 rpm has been suggested. (It is, however, believed that the initial speed aimed at was of the order of 2000 rpm.[5])

In the development of the BTM 4-rotor machine the effect on existing Bombe manufacture was minimised. The basic 3-rotor design was retained and the thirty-six fourth rotors and high-speed drives were housed in a considerable extension to the main frame. Electromatic typewriters were fitted to provide an automatic print-out of the state of rotor order and settings that produced a 'stop' condition. This became the basic configuration to which future Bombes, whether 3-rotor or 4-rotor, were built. The 4-rotor version was installed at Stanmore and Eastcote from early 1943, and shared future BTM production with 3-rotor Bombes, demand for the latter increasing during 1944. A total of 59 operational 4-rotor Bombes, serial nos. 102 to 160, was built.

The Cobra [5]

Mawdsleys of Dursley were commissioned to build the multiple arrays of high-speed rotors and BTM was asked to supply suitably modified 3-rotor Bombes, the W-W (Wynn-Williams) machines.

In August 1942 David Whitehead was a technician ('Skilled Workman') at the Folkestone Automatic Telephone Exchange and expecting his call-up into the armed services. Instead, he was asked to join a 'special job' at Dollis Hill Research Station, and was subsequently transferred to the RAF.

He joined other technicians and engineers of Tommy Flowers' group on projects for Bletchley Park. In August work began on building the prototype electronic/relay sensing and display rack for the Cobra project. As time went on most technicians were absorbed into other projects such as Colossus. But David and three others continued with Cobra until the equipment was destroyed in 1945.

The Mawdsley multiple fourth-wheel array consisted of groups of four brush holders, each with 26 radially mounted carbon brushes, positioned around a drive shaft, the carbon brushes of each holder being in contact with the periphery of a 26-segment commutator. Each group of rotors and brush holders was the equivalent of the commutator-and-rotor combination, with its four circular tracks, of a Bombe rotor position. The twelve production Cobras each consisted of 18 groups of four rotors mounted on a single drive shaft of about 16 feet long, with a centre drive motor.

The Dollis Hill equipment was assembled on a rack about 8ft high and 2ft wide. The pulse generator, which was developed as part of the measures taken to combat brush contact problems, was eventually mounted on the top of the 3-wheel Bombe. It provided the short (about 0.001 second) test pulses for the scrambler network and which were sensed by gas-filled triode valves. When a 'stop' was sensed the third and fourth wheels continued to rotate but the carry to the first and second wheels was cut. One of a bank of 26 gas-filled relays registered the output letter and another the 'stop' position of the high-speed rotor. A control panel provided an illuminated display of the input/output letter and the positions of the four rotors. A row of lever keys was provided to select an input (-80v) to one letter of the rotor network. A reset button was provided to extinguish the display and restart the carry.

Trials of the prototype Cobra took place at Stanmore in the spring of 1943 with the high-speed rotors running at 2000 rpm. Initial compatibility problems between the gas-filled valves and sensing brushes had to be overcome and the speed of the commutators was reduced to around 1200 rpm for stability, with the drive to the 3-rotor Bombe reduced accordingly. Eventually the test runs were completed with considerable success.

The Dollis Hill electronics package tested later with a prototype BTM 4-wheel Bombe was also successful. The Cobra production units were installed at Eastcote, in their own bays.[5]

Initially David Whitehead was involved with the maintenance of the Cobras, with RAF engineers maintaining the BTM Bombes, but later both teams worked on both types. He recalls

'We four PO types worked 12-hour shifts, 9 to 9, night or day, for a fortnight at a time.
'All things considered, the machines worked very well. The big electrolytic smoothing capacitors exploded from time to time. L63 triode valves developed a tendency to develop low resistance between the cathode and the grid; the 807s tended to go soft and give forth a lovely blue glow - an indication of gassiness. Others defied the 'stopper' resistances, fitted to all electrodes, and oscillated at high frequency with electrodes glowing brightly.
'I seem to remember relatively few heater or emission failures, the sort of thing one expects from valves, but they were permanently left switched on to help

preserve their life. 'Brush bounce' developed after a period of running and had to be dealt with by 'stoning' (using a carborundum stone) the commutators. This increased the amount of copper/carbon dust circulating as a result of using a powerful blower to clear the brush rotors.) The tiny carbon brushes tended to stick in their guides, which gave bad electrical contact with the commutators. The heat generated generally was considerable and resulted in tropical conditions especially in the summer.

'We were kept pretty busy throughout 1944, but in 1945 the German Naval work declined and we sometimes ran jobs on the three-wheel Bombe at normal speed with the Cobra connection replaced by a different plugboard.

'After VE Day the number of jobs rapidly dropped to zero. During the summer everything was dismantled, with much being reduced to nuts and bolts, commutator segments, and scrap metal.'

The first BTM 4-rotor Bombes were being installed at Stanmore and Eastcote from June 1943 until the end of the European war. BTM was building Bombes to the new design and, later in 1944 when the demand for 4-rotor versions slackened, was able to revert easily to assembling more 3-rotor versions.

It is believed that during the development period in 1943 comparative speed trials were undertaken between the BTM 4-rotor Bombe and the Cobra, probably at Stanmore. There was, it is believed, little difference in the actual output times between the two.*

During subsequent operation the BTM 4-wheel Bombes suffered similar maintenance problems to the Cobra. (*See* Chapter 6.)

Regarding the installations at Eastcote, David Whitehead recalls

---

* The similar performance was possibly because the 3-rotor Bombe used by the Cobras had, originally, a machine cycle of 39 index points. The Keen machine had, effectively, a faster 28-point cycle which compensated for the higher speed of the Cobra 4th rotors.

'that ten of the Eastcote bays, of which there were twelve altogether, were named after Allied countries; as best as I can reconstruct them, they and their contents were as follows:

- UNITED STATES – Standard Bombes
- CHINA – Six four-wheel Cobras
- POLAND – Six Cobras
- BELGIUM – Eight high-speed, four-wheel 'Tabs' (BTM) Bombes and six standard Bombes
- FRANCE – Fourteen 'Jumbo' Bombes with printers (for 'weak' menus)*
- GREECE – Fourteen standard Bombes
- HOLLAND – Fourteen standard Bombes
- NORWAY – Fourteen standard Bombes
- YUGOSLAVIA – Fourteen standard Bombes
- RUSSIA - Fourteen standard Bombes
- (Un-named) – Lecture room and telephone switchboard; later Americans' offices and teleprinter

As early as February 1941 an exchange of technical information took place between the British and the Americans. The Americans exchanged their reconstruction of the Japanese diplomatic cipher machine for information about BP's Enigma cryptanalysis. Four Americans spent several weeks at BP, and while there took copious notes of the Bombes and were given free access to any information they wished.[7]

In 1942, as a result of a closer collaboration, Lieutenant Joseph Eachus of the US Naval Reserve was sent to BP from the US Navy communication intelligence section. He was a mathematician and had taken a course in cryptology. For several months while at BP he studied British cryptanalysis, reported back to his US section, and assisted in codebreaking.[8] He returned to the US at the end of 1942 and took with him current BTM

---

* A standard 3-rotor Bombe with a device of relays and a multi-selector which checked at each Stop whether the sensed stecker letter was consistent. If so, the Stop was valid and the conditions printed out; if it were not, the Stop was ignored. This check minimised the number of invalid test results.

engineering drawings plus unspecified 'hardware'; these were provided by BTM in response to a directive from the British Foreign Office.[9] It is assumed that the drawings concerned included those of the 4-rotor Bombe that Doc Keen was in the process of developing and that the 'hardware' probably included, amongst other items, a sample of the 4-rotor scrambler system.*

The US Navy soon announced the development of its own 4-rotor machine with which they would deal with the U-boat Enigma. These American Bombes were built at the National Cash Register Company of Dayton, Ohio.[10] They were not in operation until several months after the British 4-rotor Bombe appeared.[11]

---

*David Whitehead states that details of the prototype Cobra high-speed rotors were also provided to the Americans.

— Chapter 8 —

Fruits of Toil, 1943 – 1973

From 1943 onward BTM, highly organised for full production of Bombes, was supplying 4-rotor versions only and these were being installed at the Stanmore and Eastcote sites. By 1944, however, U-boat activity was diminishing and pressure on the 4-rotor Bombe activity easing, and effort was increasingly being diverted to 3-rotor Bombe manufacture because of the increased activity of European keynets during the period leading up to the Allied invasion of Europe.

Manufacture and installation of CANTAB machines continued until May 1945, at the surrender of Germany and the end of the European war, when production was terminated. Finally by that time over two hundred CANTAB machines had been built and installed.

When production was terminated BTM was told to destroy all machines in the process of assembly, all components and also the thousands of engineering drawings which were in the company's possession.

During the previous August of 1944 when the end of the European war was in sight the Chairman, Ralegh Phillpotts, received a letter of appreciation from the Admiralty:

Admiralty, S.W.1.
16th August 1944

Secret.

Sir,
   I am commanded by My Lords Commissioners of the Admiralty to convey to you the mark of their appreciation of the rapid and efficient production by your company of 'CANTAB' machines and other special devices for the use of this department.

2. I am to inform you that these machines have been put to good use with results of the very highest value

to the successful prosecution of the war.

3. My Lords understand that the fine achievement of your Company in this field has in great measure been due to the work of Mr. Keen and I am to request that their appreciation of his efforts be brought to his notice.

I am, Sir,
Your obedient Servant

H. V. Markham

With the CANTAB project now terminated the whole company effort was to be redirected to its commercial business; probably around a third of the company's resources had eventually been committed to the project during the second phase of Bombe production from 1942 onward. The large number of company staff who had been working on the project, in one way or another, would be dispersed to other duties. Many of those engineers from outside BTM who had worked through the war either installing or maintaining the many Bombes would join BTM staff; some were to join the, eventually to be expanded, R & D Department.

In May 1945 the Director of GCHQ, by then Sir Edward Travis, wrote to Doc Keen:

24th May, 1945.
Dear Keen

Ever since my recent return from abroad I have been meaning to get into touch with you, not for once to ask you to undertake some momentous job in an impossible space of time, but to thank you and your gallant band of experts and workers for the outstanding assistance they have rendered to this Department of His Majesty's Government.

I did intend to get over to Letchworth to see you to tell you and your people in person that your efforts have been crowned with complete success and that this user department could not have fulfilled its duty without your sustained support including, in a recent crisis, the operation of a machine on our behalf with significant success. But since some of your staff may now be dispersing to other tasks and I must devote myself to so many problems of reorganisation, I am writing you this personal letter and asking you to pass on to all those concerned at Letchworth my sincere appreciation of their work. I know that they have often given up their spare time to see the job through and that however severe our demands have been, they have never failed us.

I still hope before long to call on you if only for a short time but feel that some word and thanks for such good service should not be any longer delayed.

Yours sincerely
Travis.

At some time between late 1944 and early 1945, before the war in Europe had come to an end, Bletchley Park was visited by Winston Churchill. His first visit had been made in September 1941 during which he made his 'geese that laid the golden eggs' reference to BP.

From the earliest days he had insisted on receiving decoded Enigma messages personally and had responded immediately to BP's 1941 appeal for increased support funds, priority supplies and the expansion of Bombe production at BTM. He had responded with an 'Action This Day' decree. But he made this last visit to thank the enormous staff at BP and the many others who had contributed to its success throughout the war.

Harold Keen was one who attended the gathering, where he was introduced to Churchill by Travis as 'the designer and builder of our Bombes'. In the King's Birthday Honours of May 1945 he was awarded the OBE for his services, and his associate, Herbert Morton, was awarded the MBE.

Later the Chairman, Mr Ralegh Phillpotts, received a Knighthood. In a subsequent letter to Doc Keen he noted that the Knighthood he had received was in recognition of the war effort of the whole company. He also remarked that in the long list of awards there were very few companies in the country that were similarly honoured.

After the war Harold Keen headed BTM's newly enlarged Research & Design department and concentrated on the development of the company's Hollerith equipment, which had remained dormant throughout the War.

In February 1946 he joined a small team headed by the Managing Director and sailed in the *Queen Elizabeth* to New York, for discussions with IBM concerning the future association between the two companies. During the visit the team members, guests of the IBM President, attended the dinner at the Waldorf-Astoria Hotel held in honour of Winston Churchill, on the occasion of his Fulton speech.

In 1949 the long-standing agreement between BTM and IBM was terminated. BTM were no longer to have free rights to future IBM patents – which had been the essence of their original agreement in 1902 – but the many existing patents were to remain completely free of royalties. Doc Keen advised the loss of patent rights to be a premature decision since by this action BTM had cut itself off from IBM's very considerable R&D at the very moment that electronic accounting machines and computers would call for unprecedented financial and technical resources.[1]

He paid two more visits to the USA: in the spring of 1953 and in November 1954, when there was still a limited relationship with IBM; between these visits came a joint BP visit to Germany.

By 1951 all the long-standing board members of BTM had died or retired. Under a new board Doc Keen commenced the development of new competitive equipment. But computers were now inevitably to supersede the long era of both punched-card technology and of Doc Keen. He eventually retired in 1959 at the age of sixty-five after 44 years with the Company. He retired with his wife Eva to Tring, and finally moved to Croxley Green, near Rickmansworth.

During 1973 he was approached by a publisher with a view to producing an account of his work on the CANTAB Project. He rejected the proposal, offering as his reason the 'thirty-year rule' within the terms of the Official Secrets Act, which would demand continuing silence for several more years. However, before any such publication could be further considered, Doc Keen died suddenly in the same year at his home in Croxley Green at the age of 79 years.

— Postscript —

By 1958 BTM had completely severed their long relationship with IBM and joined forces with Powers Samas to form International Computers & Tabulators, ICT.

In 1968 International Computers Limited, ICL, was created. Companies such as English Electric, Plessey, and Ferranti, as well as the Government, became major shareholders. The computer was rapidly replacing the Hollerith punched-card accounting system, which had lasted for sixty years.

During the following twenty or so years ICL gradually withdrew, firstly, from the manufacture of computer peripheral equipment, and later from the manufacture of computers, eventually becoming a computer services company owned by the Japanese Fujitsu. In 2001 ICL lost its separate identity and was completely absorbed into that same company.

— Appendix 1 —

The Probable Word

A particular part of an enciphered message used as a 'Probable Word' was that part thought to represent a commonly used 'clear' word, ranging from an army rank, date etc, to a phrase e.g. an address or location of an army unit. The letters of the assumed 'clear' word or phrase were aligned with the likely portion of the enciphered text. If three or more pairs of the aligned letters could be linked together by like letters into a sequence forming a 'closed loop' this became the basis for testing the validity of the assumed 'Probable Word' text and could then lead to the discovery of the initial Enigma settings that had produced the complete message, and so enable the message to be deciphered on a similarly set-up machine.

Turing required at least three closed loops for a reasonably valid test but even so they could result in an unsatisfactory level of false test results.

The following might represent a section of *supposed* clear text entered by a sequence of 20 keystrokes into an Enigma. Each clear text letter is aligned with its presumed enciphered letter. (English is used for clarity.)

Key	1	2	3	4	5	6	7	8	9	10	11	12	13	14	15	16	17	18	19	20
Clear	D	I	S	T	R	I	C	T	C	O	M	M	I	S	S	I	O	N	E	R
Cipher	F	K	Y	N	S	L	X	W	E	M	I	S	T	O	P	N	Q	S	A	N

The Probable Word key entries 1 - 20 are needed for all possible closed loops for which the relative key entry positions need to be retained. One such closed loop is formed by letter pairs at:

        key entry 10   clear O   cipher M

        key entry 12   clear M   cipher S

        key entry 14   clear S   cipher O

The loop is closed by key entry 14, cipher letter 'O' being linked to key entry 10 clear letter 'O', and overall might be expressed by the notation:

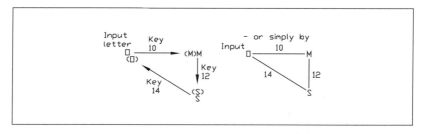

Figure 10: Notation for a closed loop.

The action of the Enigma scrambler at each of the key entries of the loop might be expressed as follows:

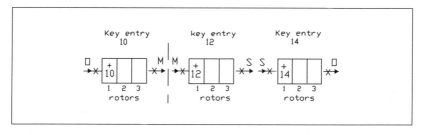

Figure 11: The Enigma scrambler closed loop sequence.
Note 1: These are three states of the one Enigma scrambler
Note 2: At key entry 1 the rotor settings are unknown, but
at entry 10, rotor 1 has advanced 10 steps,
at entry 12, rotor 1 has advanced 2 further steps, and
at entry 14, rotor 1 has advanced 2 more steps.
Note 3: The clear letter input and its cipher letter are shown at each key entry.
Note 4: X represents a possible stecker substitution for the key entry letter before input to the scrambler, and similarly a stecker substitution for the scrambler exit letter. (See Fig. 1 in Chapter 1.)

The Bombe test for a Probable Word requires more than one closed loop, but the test procedure can be demonstrated with the one closed loop shown.
The test needs to find (a) the settings of the rotors that give the closed loop condition and (b) the order of the

rotors used. The rotor settings of the Enigma scrambler at each key entry are applied to three Bombe scramblers (e.g. of nos. 10, 12 and 14) and their inputs and outputs are connected in the same closed loop sequence. For the three Bombe scramblers

a) All rotor 1, 2, 3 settings for key entry 1 are assumed to be (say) AAA.*

b) Scrambler 10 rotors 1, 2, 3 are set to JAA (J being 9 steps from AAA), scrambler 12 rotors 1, 2, 3 are set to LAA (L being 11 steps from AAA) and scrambler 14 rotors 1, 2 3, to NAA (N being 13 steps from AAA).

The three Bombe scramblers are then run in unison through the 26 x 26 x 26 positions of each rotor order to search for the settings that produce the closed loop. At the same time, one possible letter substitution by the steckerboard is determined as an integral part of the procedure.

In Fig. 11 (the closed loop condition), the link between key entries is a common letter, whether a stecker substitution exists on either side of it, or not. In either case the scrambler output letter is identical to the next input letter to the scrambler.** When the rotors of the Bombe scramblers reach the same order and settings, any stecker substitutions are also irrelevant and are therefore ignored throughout the test, the interconnections being made directly between their inputs and outputs.

The exception is in the return link between scramblers 14 and 10. This link will be used for a test to establish either the true letter 'O', or a substitution letter. This test, and also the complete verification of the closed loop, is initiated by the insertion of a trial letter into the return link. The test (with its outcome) is a function of the Register.

---

* The settings used for Key entry 1 are arbitrary since during the Bombe test all possible rotor settings will be tested. AAA might be a logical choice.
** If letter A is steckered to M, then letter M is reciprocally steckered to A.

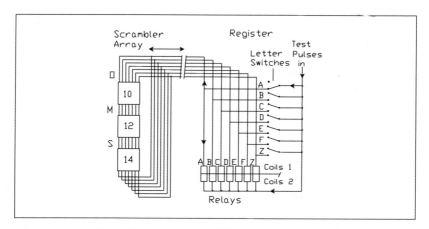

Figure 12: The Turing closed loop test.
(Using one closed loop only. For clarity, the A-Z lines and switches are represented by seven lines only.)

The Register comprises 26 (A-Z) relays to store the test result at each rotor-3 position. In Figure 6a each relay has differentially wired coils 1 and 2. Energising either coil separately will operate the relay, both energised together will not.

To determine any possible stecker-substituted letter for 'O' a trial letter is entered. The 26 (A-Z) inputs of scrambler 10 are connected to a set of A-Z switches. The trial stecker letter, e.g. 'A', is selected by switch 'A' which will feed a test pulse to scrambler 10 on its A-line input and will also energise the A relay coil-1. At the same time the pulse will energise all coils-2.

The scramblers are driven through all 26 x 26 x 26 rotor positions by continuously turning rotors-3 in unison and passing carries to their rotors 2 and 1.
At each index point of the rotors-3 cycle, a test pulse is sent to scrambler 10 input 'A', passes through the loop and exits from scrambler 14.

  a) If at a particular position, all rotor settings are correct for a closed-loop condition and if the trial stecker letter 'A' is correct, the pulse will find a single path through the scrambler loop and exit the 'A' line and no other. The input pulse will also energise the 'A' relay coil-1 directly, and simultaneously energise all relay coils-2. Relay 'A' will therefore *not* operate, but relays B-Z will, by means of their coils-2.

b) If there is no closed-loop condition the pulse will recirculate random paths on all 26 lines through the scramblers and energise all A-Z relay coils-1. Since all coils-2 are also energised *no* relays are operated.

c) When a closed-loop condition exists but the steckered letter for 'O' is other than the trial input 'A', the test pulse will re-circulate scramblers on all lines except that of the true stecker letter, for example 'B', and will energise all relay coils-1 *except* that of relay 'B'. *Only* relay 'B' will be operated, by its coil-2.

Results (a) or (c) will activate a STOP and suspend the test. The three rotor types used, their order of mounting and their particular settings are noted. The stecker substitution letter for 'O' is also required and so the state of the relays is made externally visible with a visual Indicator Unit of 26 A-Z positions, each position being tripped by its register relay.

The Enigma settings indicated might then be applied to an Enigma-type machine and the closed-loop keyed letters entered, conforming to their relative entry positions in the Probable Word, and the closed loop possibly reproduced and verified. Verification of the complete Probable Word might follow and the remaining stecker substitution letters rationally deduced.

The Turing test with three closed loops

Key	1	2	3	4	5	6	7	8	9	10	11	12	13	14	15	16	17	18	19	20
Clear	D	I	S	T	R	I	C	T	C	O	M	M	I	S	S	I	O	N	E	R
Cipher	F	K	Y	N	S	L	X	W	E	M	I	S	T	O	P	N	Q	S	A	N

The twenty-position clear text and its cipher text contain a number of links including those forming three closed loops as shown below:

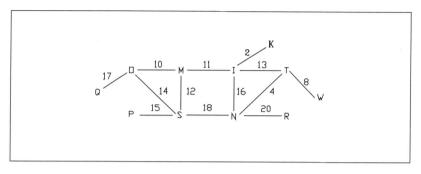

Figure 13: A MENU showing closed loops and letter pairs.

If a single closed loop only were used for the test of 26 x 26 x 26 (**one** order of rotors out of sixty) rotor positions it could result in signalling (falsely) a similar number of closed loops.

The number of false signals might vary inversely with the number of closed loops employed. The use of three was considered a compromise between the need to minimise false signals and the limitations involved with longer Probable Word texts needed for finding extra loops.

In the example the span of the single loop is 5, and of all 3 loops together is 15, out of 20 positions of text. With this text keyed into an Enigma the input rotor would step through 20 of its 26 positions with a likelihood of passing a carry to rotor 2 and distorting the subsequent Bombe test. So the span of text positions used had to be kept to a minimum. A carry-over might possibly be avoided by further Bombe runs with the starting position of the rotor settings moved.[1]

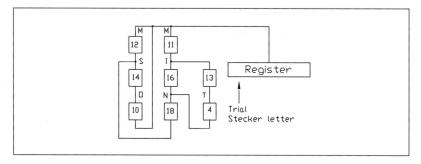

Figure 14: A 3-closed loop configuration.
Note: Each single line used for connections between scramblers and Register represents a cable of 26 a-z lines.

The trial stecker letter might be entered by the test pulse on cable 'M' at the junction of the first and second loops where there are three entry channels into the scramblers. An apparently valid test result requires a simultaneous closed-loop condition in all three loops, with the test pulse finding a single track through all three, or else 25 out of 26 tracks. But the rate of false signals encountered when using three loops remained excessive, and the time involved in off-line re-checking was considered impracticable.

The Diagonal Board

The diagonal board exploited the reciprocal steckering inherent in the Enigma steckerboard where, e.g., if 'M' were steckered to 'A' then 'A' would be steckered to 'M'. In addition, by using letter pairs as well as closed loops, more scrambler connections were possible. As a result the majority of the remaining false Stops were nullified.

Each scrambler input and output letter may be a steckered letter substitution of either a clear or a cipher letter. If 'a' is the stecker letter on the 'M' cable into scrambler 12, then 'm' is the reciprocal stecker letter on a possible cable 'A'. The diagonal board provides this reciprocal connection. If this connection joins an existing valid test path it will have no effect; but if the true stecker

73

of 'M' is a letter other than 'a' then the connection will create an additional path, and possibly multiple paths, through the scramblers, considerably reducing the possibility of a false closed-loop signal. The use of letter pairs reduced the number of closed loops needed, and allowed shorter Probable Word texts, markedly reducing the likelihood of a carry-over occurring.

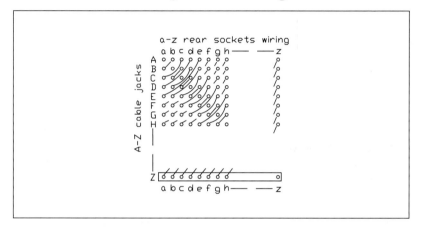

Figure 15: The diagonal board.

The diagonal board is an array of twenty-six 26-way jacks. Each jack has 26 sockets to which the connecting cables between scramblers and/or Register, with their 26 a-z lines, may be plugged, commoning jacks being provided for multiple connection.

The rear of the sockets of the 26 jacks are cross-wired to effect the reciprocal stecker connections. For example, the 'a' socket of the 'M' cable jack is wired to the 'm' socket of the 'A' cable jack and so on. (A test pulse on line 'a' in the 'M' cable connector would then be passed on to the 'm' line in cable 'A', creating a new path if connection cable 'A' were in use.)

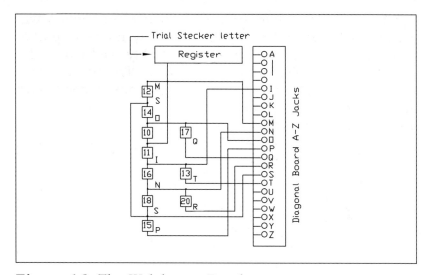

Figure 16: The Welchman Bombe.
A combination of closed loops, 3 letter-pairs and a diagonal board.

After a likely Probable Word with sufficient loops and linked pairs had been established at BP a MENU would be compiled detailing the Bombe settings necessary for a test.

The MENU would include, with other items, the scrambler positions, rotor order and settings to be used, interconnections between Register, scramblers and diagonal board, and the entry of the input letter. In a MENU these would be shown in a form of notation similar to that used above.

In Chapter 6 it was noted that BTM formed teams of engineers to install or rehabilitate any Bombe at any of the installation sites. A surviving notebook kept by one such team member, Frank Keen*, during February 1945 contains details of overall function tests carried out on a 4-rotor Bombe, number 104, at Stanmore. It includes examples of machine set-up examinations and

---

* The author's elder brother, who was closely involved with CANTAB development over 5 years, and probably knew as much about the Bombe as anyone.

correction, and of final operational tests, the latter including a number of specific MENU applications that were used.

Below is one example of a MENU recorded which shows a number of closed loops and links within fourteen positions of an encryption and a related Probable Word:

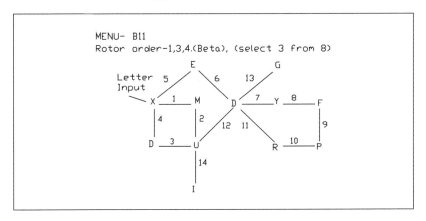

Figure 17: A MENU for a 4-rotor Bombe, 1944.

The 'crib' covers a span of only 14 positions of text yet contains three closed loops, of 4 and 5 letter pairs, plus two separate letter pairs.

Note: 'Beta' was the first 4th-rotor introduced for the U-boat Enigma. In July 1943 the Germans introduced a second alternative version, 'Gamma'. No issue of an 'Alpha' version has been recorded.

— Appendix 2 —

The Enigma Era

In the spring of 1918 a thirty-nine-year-old German electrical engineer named Arthur Scherbius informed the Imperial Navy of his application for a patent for a cipher machine based on multiple rotors. He extolled its security virtues and enclosed details hoping for their interest. The Navy rejected his machine and so did the German Foreign Office.[1]

Scherbius was interested in cryptology and had dabbled with cipher machines based on the rotor and, significantly, was one of the first to introduce electrical operation. He and his associate, E Richard Ritter, had already formed a company, Scherbius & Ritter, in 1918, and were inventing many items of a technical nature. Scherbius was particularly noted for the publicised 'Scherbius Principle for Asynchronous Motors'.

Scherbius and his associate transferred the patent rights to a commercial company, Gewerkschaft Securitas who later founded 'Chiffriermaschinen Aktiengesellschaft' in 1923 in which they themselves became Directors.

This company developed the machine into the basic form which became known as Enigma. It comprised three rotors and a reversing commutator, the *Umkehrwalze*, which reflected the current back through the rotors. This feature was never altered.

Typewriter-key entries caused the rotors to be stepped through their rotation providing an ever-changing substitution of entry letters. It caused much publicity when manufactured and exhibited in 1923 for use primarily by commercial companies. In 1924 the German Post Office exchanged Enigma-enciphered greetings with the International Postal Union; it did not, however, attract much commercial interest.[2]

Eventually in 1926 the company produced a small batch of the machines for the German navy, each having five different rotors from which three were selected for insertion into the machine. In 1928 the Enigma went into service with the army, and during subsequent years the device was continuously developed and its security improved, but Scherbius died in 1929 before the full success of his machine was realised.

In 1930 secret negotiations with the army were concluded; a military version was constructed and the 'Steckerboard' was introduced which vastly increased the number of possible cipher combinations and hence its overall security.[3]

In 1935 Germany denounced the Versailles treaty, which had placed limits on her armed forces after the defeat in the First World War, and expanded her armed forces. Enigma had been adopted in 1933-4 as the basic cipher system for the sophisticated radio communication system used by all the armed services, military intelligence, the SS and all political intelligence services.[4]

By 1934 the German navy had adopted the superior army Enigma but opted for seven rotors from which to select three for use, the extra two being for communications within the navy. It then divided its cipher communications into two nets, one using a home waters key, and one a foreign waters key.[5]

In September 1938, prior to the Munich conference, some 20,000 Enigmas were being used by the German army, air force, navy, and leading civil agencies. By the end of the month varying degrees of mobilisation were taking place in Germany, Czechoslovakia, France and Italy.[6]

By mid-summer 1939, the number of Enigmas in use doubled to an estimated 40,000.[7]

During the 1920s and 1930s many of the nations which had been involved in the First War had established cryptanalytic agencies. Poland, which had not gained cryptanalysis experience during the war, had regained statehood and now learned quickly in order to retain and protect it, and eventually created a Cipher Bureau which became superior to those of other nations.[8]

The Polish Cipher Bureau in the early 1930s was the first such department to engage mathematicians to study cryptology. Those who were recruited from Poznan University also knew German as the language was in common use there. They were methodically instructed in cryptology and the three who were selected, Rejewski, Rozycki and Zygalski, became full-time cryptologists in 1932.[9]

Rejewski was set aside to study the Enigma. Soon after making preliminary investigations of intercepted Enigma messages he was given a *commercial* Enigma acquired in Germany.

During 1931 and 1932 French Military Intelligence acquired valuable documents concerning the *military* Enigma. These were passed to the Polish Bureau and the details that Rejewski eventually received contained examples of Enigma-enciphered messages of the German forces together with the German usage procedures and a copy of the monthly tables of army keys for the year 1932. With this information, together with his highly mathematical approach, he was able to deduce the wiring of the right-hand rotor.

Since the rotor order in the keys changed quarterly he was able to deduce the wiring of the remaining two rotors as they each in turn appeared in the right-hand position. This enabled him to discover the details of all three rotors in use, their settings and the German operating procedures.[10]

Eventually, in 1933, the Cipher Bureau had sufficient design details to commission the small and specialised AVA Radio Manufacturing Company of Warsaw to manufacture a number of copies of the military Enigma machine.

AVA had begun life in 1927 as a one-room radio workshop. The owner, Fokczynski, was known to the Cipher Bureau and occasionally received commissions from it. Between 1929 and 1932 his modest shop was transformed into AVA, a specialised manufacturing firm, founded by himself and three others, one of whom was a full-time employee of the Bureau engaged on German ciphers and who had once been a lecturer on cryptology at Poznan University. The remaining two were radio enthusiasts from Warsaw Polytechnic.

During the early 1930s AVA, then in new buildings and employing up-to-date technology, became closely associated with the Bureau which had begun ordering radio communication equipment from them. By 1932 AVA became the first industrial plant in Poland to have its production processes put on a scientific basis. By 1934 the company had manufactured over a dozen Enigma copies.[11]

In 1936 AVA designed and manufactured the components for the 'Cyclometer', consisting of two linked sets of Enigma rotors and, finally, in 1938, the company produced the components of six 'Bomby' for assembly at the Bureau.

In January 1938 a fortnight's survey of the efficiency of the Bureau, carried out by the Polish General Staff, found that the ten-man team of cryptologists and operators were able to solve and read 75% of all intercepted Enigma messages.[12]

The AVA Company also manufactured the Bureau-designed Polish cipher machine called 'Lacida', unknown to Rejewski and others, for use by the Polish higher commands in the event of war.[13]

In June 1939 the German Army issued a document 'Instructions for Wartime Radio Traffic' about a change in cipher keys as of 1 July; at the same time a huge issue of Enigma machines was made to German combat units. A re-issue of the June directive was made on 2 August and would become operative when the code word 'Molch' was broadcast. This took place on 31 August. The next day Germany invaded Poland and World War II began.

On 1 September 1939 the first German air raids on Warsaw occurred and hit the new AVA manufacturing plant. These buildings had been built and re-equipped shortly before the war.[14]

In mid-September Rejewski and his team were told

to leave Warsaw and re-form at an alternative place, but on 17 September the Red Army had advanced into Poland from the east and the cryptologists were told to destroy their equipment and documents and cross into Romania.[15] The cipher team was evacuated out of the country. At least three Enigma copies, and two Lacidas, eventually arrived in France with the team and during 1940 the latter were used for enciphering messages between the French Intelligence centre and London.

The Poles joined the French cryptologists at Bruno who, in the early months of 1940, had received copies of the 'Jeffreys Sheets' from the British Government Code & Cipher School at Bletchley Park in Buckinghamshire and had shared in breaking Enigma messages until the German invasion of France and the fall of Paris. Evacuation to Algeria followed and then their rejoining the French cryptologists in Vichy-France. Finally, in 1943, with France completely overrun, the cryptologists, including Rejewski, arrived in England. There they were not allowed to join Bletchley Park permanently but were assigned to a signals company of the Polish forces in exile.[16]

In December 1938 the Germans had increased the number of Enigma rotors available from three to five which required ten times as many Bomby and sets of perforated sheets as before. This was beyond the resources of the Poles at the time when war with Germany was inevitable. Just before the invasion of their country on 1 September 1939, the Poles handed all the details of their Enigma-breaking activities to their allies, the French and the British, the latter using these straight away at Bletchley Park.

Soon after, during the autumn of 1939, BTM became the major commercial engineering company critically involved with the cryptologists of Bletchley Park, and thus in the resolution of the problems created by Enigma.

As early as 1941 Bletchley Park cryptologists, in their turn, were already imparting their own knowledge and experience of cryptology to the USA and, eventually, this included full details of the British Bombe.

By the autumn of 1942 and early 1943 the USA had been given the design details of the 4-rotor Bombe. By the late summer of 1943 American 4-rotor Bombes were being built at the National Cash Register Company at Dayton, Ohio. These US Bombes were operated by US Navy WAVES personnel at the Mount Vernon Seminary in Washington, mainly on the U-Boat Enigma traffic.[17]

In 1935 the Air Ministry supervised the construction and distribution of the British Typex machine which was based on the Enigma (and in violation of its patent) and the Creed Teleprinter Company contributed to its design.[18] It was used by the army and the RAF, but not by the Admiralty nor the Foreign Office.[19]

It was used later at Bletchley Park, suitably modified, to simulate the Enigma machine and used for verifying 'Stops' which occurred during a Bombe run, and also for the transposing back to plain (German) language the deciphered Enigma messages once their rotor settings were known.

Later during the war years the Powers Samas Company of Croydon also manufactured large numbers of Typex machines.[20]

The Germans had complete faith in the invulnerability of their cipher machine. It is believed that they had captured several Typex machines during the British withdrawal from Dunkirk in 1940, and had recognised Typex as a copy of their own Enigma. As such they probably assumed it had a similar high security and therefore it would be time wasted for them to study Typex message intercepts.[21]

At the end of the war some fifty Bombes were retained at Eastcote, the new GCHQ location. They were almost immediately put to work, presumably on Eastern Bloc ciphers. Some of these machines were to be stored away but others were required to run new jobs and sixteen were kept comparatively busy on Menus.[22]

It has been suggested by some that the reason for the continued secrecy surrounding the Bletchley Park operation, and the method of reading Enigma encipherments, was to enable the British to market captured Enigma machines in some countries as valid, secure, encryption machines.[23]

The majority of the Bombes were destroyed in 1945, including all those at BTM in the process of assembly, all components and many engineering drawings.

However, not all the engineering drawings were destroyed, some being retained by GCHQ, and others in the USA, as a result of the earlier exchanges. Some three thousand drawings were recovered from GCHQ by the Bletchley Park Trust to be used for the major Bombe Rebuild programme in BP's Hut 11.

— Major published sources —

*In the Notes & References which follow
these are referred to by authors' surnames only.*

Campbell-Kelly, Martin. *ICL: a business and technical history.*
Oxford University Press, 1989.

Garlinski, Jozef. *Intercept: the Enigma war.*
London: Dent, 1979.

Hinsley, F H, & Stripp, Alan. *Codebreakers: the inside story of
Bletchley Park.* Oxford University Press, 1993.

Hodges, Andrew. *Alan Turing: the enigma of intelligence.*
London: Unwin Hyman, 1987.

Kahn, David. *Seizing the Enigma: the race to break the German
U-Boat codes, 1939-1943.* London: Souvenir, 1992.

Kozaczuk, Wladyslaw. *Enigma: how the German machine cipher
was broken, and how it was read by the Allies in World
War Two.* London: Arms & Armour Press, 1984.

Smith, Michael. *Station X: the codebreakers of Bletchley Park.*
London: Channel 4, 1998.

Welchman, Gordon. *The Hut Six Story: breaking the Enigma
codes.* Cleobury Mortimer: Baldwin, 1997 (revised edition).

West, Nigel. *GCHQ: the secret wireless war, 1900-86.*
London: Weidenfeld & Nicolson, 1986.

Whitehead, David J. 'Cobra and Other Bombes'. *Cryptologia,*
Vol 20, No 4, 1994.

— Notes & References —

Chapter 1: Formative Years, 1894 - 1939
1 Campbell-Kelly, p 8.   2 *Ibid.,* p 8.
3 *Ibid.,* p 16.   4 *Ibid.,* p 5.
5 *Ibid.,* p 27.   6 *Ibid.,* p 34.
7 *Ibid.,* p 50.   8 *Ibid.,* p 90.

Chapter 2: Enigma
1 Kozaczuk, p xiii.   2 West, p 129.
3 Kozaczuk, p 48.   4 *Ibid.,* p 61.
5 Garlinski, p 194.

Chapter 3: The Polish Codebreakers
1 Kozaczuk, p 9.   2 *Ibid.,* pp 17-19.
3 Kahn, pp 62-66.   4 Kozaczuk, p 25.
5 *Ibid.,* pp 29 and 263.   6 *Ibid.,* p 53.
7 *Ibid.,* p 54.
8 Ibid., p 63. 'Production of sixty cryptological bombs would
   have cost an estimated 1.5 million *złotych* (then about
   $350,000). Yet the funds provided for new projects and
   development of radio intelligence, in the Cipher Bureau's
   budget for fiscal year 1937-38, did not exceed 100,000
   złotych, or some $23,000.'
9 Kahn, pp 78-81.

Chapter 4: Bletchley Park
1 Kahn, pp 86, 87, 93-5, and Hodges, p 176. After the Allied
   meeting with the Poles on July 24 & 25, at which the
   Allies received full details of the Polish work on Enigma,
   the Poles each received a set of similar batons from
   GC&CS as tokens of appreciation. (Kozaczuk, p 60.)
2 The contemporary value of the CANTAB contract (for the
   design and manufacture of the original batch of 70
   Bombes) had been £100,000. (Smith, p 52.)

Chapter 5: Doc Keen and CANTAB

1   Kahn, p 99.
2   Hodges, p 184.
    'But there was nothing simple about the construction of
    such a machine. To be of practical use, a Bombe would
    have to work through an average of half a million rotor
    positions in hours rather than days, which meant that the
    logical process would have to be applied to at least twenty
    positions every second. This was within the range of auto-
    matic telephone exchange equipment, which could
    perform switching operations in a thousandth of a
    second. But unlike the relays of telephone exchanges, the
    Bombe components would have to work continuously and
    in concert, for hours at a stretch, with the rotors moving
    in perfect synchrony. Without the solution of these
    engineering problems, in a time that would normally see
    no more than a rough blueprint prepared, all the logical
    ideas would have been idle dreams.'
3   Welchman, p 81:
    'Although I did not realize it then, Harold "Doc" Keen of
    the British Tabulating Machine Company, which was
    associated with IBM in America, must already have
    started on the design of the Turing bombe. Travis asked
    me to work closely with Keen, and this started what was
    to become both a close collaboration and a close
    friendship. Keen soon grasped the new idea and set to
    work on two prototype bombes incorporating the diagonal
    board. The design proved to be extremely flexible, quite
    adaptable to changes as they became necessary.'
    And p 241: The diagonal board 'is simply a 26 x 26 matrix
    of terminals. It acquired its name because, for example,
    the terminal in row E and column A is connected
    diagonally to the terminal in row A and column E. The
    cross-connection is no more than an electrical equivalent
    of the fact that, if E is steckered to A, then A must be
    steckered to E. I believe that the name 'diagonal board'
    was introduced by Doc Keen.'

Chapter 6: The Bombe Makers

1   Welchman, p 138:
    'This was a remarkable achievement, for it had taken a lot
    of skilled design, careful planning of manufacturing

procedure, and a vast expenditure of general effort to turn mere ideas into complex operating machinery. . . . it was not long before bombes from the production line began to arrive. John Monroe remembers that when he arrived in June 1941 we already had four to six bombes, including the prototypes. Harold Fletcher believes that we had eight to twelve bombes by the time he arrived on August 6, 1941. So it seems that Doc Keen was already delivering production models at the rate of around three per month. That the bombes performed so satisfactorily says a great deal for their basic design and manufacture. They had to operate twenty-four hours a day, seven days a week, month after month, and then year after year. Their only "time off" was the few hours during which they received their regular servicing by the RAF mechanics. Breakdowns were not nearly so frequent as might have been anticipated considering their unique nature and how quickly they had had to be developed.'

2 Welchman, p 139.   3   *Ibid.,* p 124.
4 *Ibid.,* pp 139-141.   5   *Ibid.,* p 141.
6 Whitehead, pp 305-306.
7 Welchman, pp 145-6.   8   Kahn, p 235.

Chapter 7: The Fourth Rotor

1 Kahn, p 184.   2   *Ibid.,* pp 189-190.
3 *Ibid.,* pp 201-202, 205, 209.   4   Hodges, pp 223-224.
5 Whitehead, pp 289-297.
6 Items recorded by Frank Keen in 1945 relating to rotor-4 speed include:

a) A pulse-generator circuit, using five gas-filled triode switching pairs which appear to generate a sequence of five pulses during the +ve going edge of a 50-cycle AC voltage. These, combined with pulses from a second circuit whose 50-cycle AC source has a 180° phase shift, might provide a pulse stream of 500 pulses per second to trigger a power valve (indicated) to generate test pulses.

   To use 500p/sec test pulses synchronised with the rotor-4 cycle, the rotor speed would need to be 1154 rpm and the 50-cycle AC voltages might require to be generated by an alternator (or alternators) integrated with the rotor drives.

b) On rotor-4, the brushes of rows 1 and 3, and of rows 2 and 4, and, by inference, similarly the segments of related commutator rows, are wired together. This, effectively, provides two rows of brushes/segments instead of four. The brushes of rows 1 and 3, and of 2 and 4, are differentially adjusted to extend the overall brush/segment duration of the combina- tion (perhaps to 0.8 of an Index point) which allows test pulses of longer duration and hence an increase in rotor speed.

    The total rotor-4 circuitry would be a combination of the rotor internal wiring plus the umkehrwalze wiring, before connecting to the rotor-3 return paths.

c) The rotor-4 test cycle is shown occupying 2/3 of each rotor-3 Index point.

Items (a), (b) and (c) together might suggest a possible assessment of the 4-rotor Bombe performance to be of the order of:

Rotor-4 speed = **1154 rpm**   **[1]**
Rotor-4 cycle time = 0.052 sec.
One Index point time = 0.002 sec.
Possible brush/segment path = 0.002 x 0.8 [*see* (b)]
                                    = 0.0016 sec
so a possible test pulse time = **0.001(+) sec**   **[2]**
               (sufficient for relay operation?)
Rotor-3 Index point   = 0.052 x 3/2 sec [see (c)]
                      = 0.078 sec
Rotor-3 cycle = 26 x 0.078 = 2.03 sec
Thus its speed = 29 rpm   [3]
The machine cycle (28 Index points) = 28 x 0.078 = 2.2 secs
Time to test one order of 4 rotors = 2.2 x 26 x 26/60
                                      = **24 mins**   **[4]**

7 Kahn, p 237.   8 *Ibid.,* p 238.

9   A memo, addressed to H. H. Keen in 1942:

Room 17,
Foreign Office,
S.W.1.
5th September, 1942.

Dear Mr. Keen,
It would be in order for you to hand mechanical drawings of
Cantab and parts to Lt. Eachus, U.S.N.

Signed
(signature)

10 Kahn, p 239.
11 Hodges, p 262.

Chapter 8: Fruits of Toil, 1943-1973
1   Campbell-Kelly, p 143.

Appendix 1: The Probable Word
1   Welchman, p 246. A description of methods employed to
    counter the effect of a carry-over occurring during a
    lengthy probable word.

Appendix 2: The Enigma Era

1   Kahn, p 31.   2   *Ibid.,* p 38.
3   Kozaczuk, p xiii.   4   *Ibid.*
5   Kahn, pp 43, 44.   6   Kozaczuk, pp 48, 49.
7   *Ibid.,* p 61.   8   Kahn, p 49.
9   Kozaczuk, pp 1-4.
10 Kozaczuk, pp 17, 18 and Kahn, pp 62-6.
11 Kozaczuk, p 28.   12 *Ibid.,* p 45.
13 Kozaczuk, pp 119, 135.   14 Kozaczuk, p 69.
15 Garlinski, p 56.   16 Kozaczuk, Chaps 7 & 8.
17 Kahn, p 239-40.   18 West, p 122.
19 Hodges, p 165.   20 Campbell-Kelly, p 114.
21 West, p 23.   22 Smith, p 176.
23 Welchman, p 17.

— BLETCHLEY PARK —

At the Government's Code & Cipher School at Bletchley Park, valuable work on enemy codes was carried out throughout WW2. Of immense value to the Allies was the Intelligence gained from breaking Enigma and Lorenz *Geheimschreiber* codes. By the of the war, thousands of Enigma messages were being decoded every day, and work on the Lorenz codes had led to the building of the world's first electronic computer - Colossus - in 1943.

On the site, the Bletchley Park Trust now provides a wealth of displays and exhibitions on cryptology, wireless, and other WW2 themes, including the Cryptology Trail (with hands-on Enigma operation), replica Colossus (built 1996) and the nation's largest collection of Churchill memorabilia. The site is open to the public every day from February to November, with (optional) guided tours available.

Opening times are 10.30 a.m. to 5.00 p.m. (last admissions 3.30 p.m.). Details may change, so potential visitors are advised to check first on 01908 640404 or www.bletchleypark.org.uk

—— Britain's best-kept secret ——

— The Hut Six Story —
—by—
Gordon Welchman

When the war started, Gordon Welchman, a talented mathematician, was a Fellow of Trinity College, Cambridge, and thus an obvious recruit for the expanding codebreaking operations at Bletchley Park. He worked there throughout the war, and later wrote this authoritative record of how the breaking of the Enigma ciphers was actually carried out on a day-to-day basis. No other code-breaker has left us a first-hand account of Bletchley Park, spanning the whole of the war.

Originally published in 1982, the book was out of print and difficult to find for many years. Our new edition has been corrected, and also contains the author's final thoughts on his wartime work, in the form of a paper which he did not live to see published. The book is thus a more complete and fitting tribute to a man who achieved so much for his country. One of his wartime colleagues, Sir Stuart Milner-Barry later referred to these important achievements: 'If Welchman had not been there, I doubt if Ultra [information derived from de-ciphering German Enigma messages] would have played the part it undoubtedly did in shortening the war.'

xiv + 263 pages, illustrated. Card covers.
ISBN 0 947712 34 8   £8.50

— Top Secret Ultra —
—by—
Peter Calvocoressi

Following his History First at Oxford, Peter Calvocoressi was practising as a barrister when war broke out. In 1940, he joined the RAF as an Intelligence Officer and was soon sent to Bletchley Park, where he worked to the end of the war. He later built a career in publishing, finally becoming Chief Executive of Penguin Books. He writes and lectures widely on twentieth-century history.

This account of his wartime work was originally published in 1980, but the author has extensively revised the book for our new edition, which also contains new illustrations. It remains, however, a valuable personal account of personal experience. No other book has been written by an Intelligence Officer at Bletchley, describing the work in detail.

Peter Calvocoressi worked in Hut 3, assessing the intelligence significance of the decrypted German Air Force and Army Enigma signals. He gives us an excellent overview - describing the Enigma machine and its ciphers, its breaking, the role of the Intelligence Officers, and finally offers judgements as to how this work changed the course of the war.

158 pages, illustrated. Card covers.
ISBN 0 947712 41 0   £6.50

— My Road to Bletchley Park —
—by—
Doreen Luke

Completing our trio of books written by people who actually worked at Bletchley Park during the Second World War, is this book by a Wireless Operator & Morse Slip Reader.

Doreen Luke (née Spencer) was only 15 when war broke out, and was working in a draper's shop. Her father, who had been a Signals Officer in the First World War, gave her a good grounding in Morse Code, then as soon as she turned 18, she joined the Women's Auxiliary Air Force to train as a wireless operator. In her book, she recalls vividly her months of training at various camps in England and Scotland before she was sent to Bletchley Park. Here, at the famous British codebreaking centre, she worked for the next three years in Bletchley's 'E' Block, playing an essential role in the series of stages linking the interception of the original German wireless transmissions to the production of the final intelligence, used to such effect by Allied commanders in the field.

No other book has been written by a BP wireless operator, so this remains a unique first-hand account of war-time communications at Bletchley.

53 pages, illustrated. Card covers.
ISBN 0 947712 44 5   £5

— Colossus 1943 - 1996 —
—by—
Tony Sale

Although it is the German Enigma ciphers which first come to mind when Bletchley Park is mentioned, many other codes and ciphers were tackled by the code-breakers. One of the most sophisticated codes was produced by the Lorenz *Geheimschreiber* machine. Its power was such that pencil and paper techniques were far too slow. What was needed was a new type of machine - an electronic machine - to analyse the coded messages as a first step towards recovering their meaning.

Max Newman was the man who first saw how a suitable new machine could be designed and Tommy Flowers, a brilliant Post Office Research Engineer, transformed Newman's ideas into a roomful of equipment - the world's first electronic computer - Colossus.

After the war, all ten Colossus machines were dismantled, but the first Museum Director at Bletchley Park, Tony Sale, felt that visitors should be able to see a replica of Colossus, so he undertook the amazing task of creating a full-size working replica, which is now on view at Bletchley He also wrote this brief account of the 'breaking' of the ciphers, and the building of the replica.

17 pages, illustrated. Card covers.
ISBN 0 947712 36 4   £3

— The U-Boat Commander's Handbook —

When the US Navy captured U505 off the west coast of Africa in June 1944, not only did they seize the U-Boat, but also all its equipment and documentation, including the Enigma machine and a manual of tactics - 'The U-Boat Commander's Handbook'. This was a distillation of the experience gained by the early U-Boat aces, designed to help the younger Commanders when at sea. The captured volume was translated for the use of the Allies, but not published for many years. M & M Baldwin are the sole importers of this book, which provides a unique insight into the principles of U-Boat warfare.

115 pages, illustrated. Card covers.   £7.50

— The War Diaries of U764 —
——*by*——
Heinz Guske

Normally, the only sources for the history of the individual U-Boats are the records at HQ and the Commander's *Kriegstagebuch.* However, U764's Commander deliberately distorted his reports to HQ to conceal his reckless behaviour. After the war, he wrote a boastful and inaccurate account of his war service. Little did he know that Guske, a wireless officer on U764, and therefore one of the few people in a position to know the accuracy of U764's wireless reports, was alive and living in London. We are the sole importers of this detailed analysis, in which Guske proves that the official record was falsified.

189 pages, illustrated. Card covers.   £8